# Twice a Week Heroes

Stories that skim the surface of the history of fast pitch softball in Springfield, Missouri.

# DANNY MILES

## DEDICATION

Twice A Week Heroes is dedicated to Susan Miles, the love of my life for over 35 years, and the players, wives, families, friends and fans that make up the "fastpitch family".

Copyright © 2021 Danny Miles
All cover art copyright © 2021 Danny Miles
All Rights Reserved

No part of this book may be reproduced or transmitted in any form or by any means, electronic or mechanical, including photocopying, recording, or by any information storage and retrieval system, without permission in writing from the author.

Publishing Coordinator – Sharon Kizziah-Holmes

Paperback-Press
an imprint of A & S Publishing
A & S Holmes, Inc.

ISBN -13: 978-1-951772-97-0

# INTRODUCTION

This book is a collection of stories that skims the surface of the history of fast pitch softball in Springfield, Missouri, along with the recollections of my and other's personal experiences related to the game. I began the endeavor due to the urging of Ancil (Spike) Fry who recognized that my love of the sport mirrored his own involvement and hoped that the game could be preserved in history.

The information is as factual as my limited research and somewhat dysfunctional memory might allow. I relied heavily upon the input of my brother Jim Miles and other friends and teammates who shared the journey with me.

My dear friend Nello McDaniel has provided the title as well as encouragement and direction though out the process and without his help this undertaking would probably have never been realized. Much information was gleaned from Springfield Newspapers, Inc. and the late Dave Schulty, a great sportswriter and softball fan.

Every Sunday morning's newspaper was torn apart getting to his "Thumbing Through Softball" column to see the top hitters and pitchers in the league based upon his cumulation of statistics from park board data. Springfield Parks and Softball directors Jim Ewing, Dan Kinney, Joey Rich, and Mark Nelson should be appreciated for their efforts to grow the sport and to bring many state, regional, and national tournaments to the city.

I began many inquiries with the simple question "why did fast pitch softball mean so much to you"? Most answers started basically with "it was an opportunity to compete in a sport at a high level".

Even though most of us were not at the very pinnacle of ability we were given chances to play with and against players who were national tournament level athletes and by whom we could measure our own prowess. The conversations most always ended in the expression of appreciation for the many friends, fans and acquaintances that the game allowed us to accumulate.

I think most important to everyone were the memories they have embraced and relived so many times. I came to realize just how many people share my feelings and how impactful fast pitch has been in our lives. I have discovered from my inept technological forays on the internet several websites that really opened my eyes to the wide scope of fast pitch softball's appeal. Literally thousands of players in hundreds of the nation's towns and cities competed and loved the game performed before even more adoring fans. Each of them has their own stories and hopefully they can pass those along to another generation.

Many thanks to Louie Bunch Jr. and Louie Bunch Sr., Pat and Mike Bramer, Bryan Tucker, Jeff Findley, Ben Gehler, and especially longtime respected softball foe and one time teammate John Younger of St. Joseph, Missouri for introducing me to a completely enhanced perspective.

Springfield's fast pitch softball success was always dependent upon local sponsors that footed the bill for uniforms, equipment, entry fees, and travel expenses. Recognition is justified for all of them and especially Shorty Harrison and Glen Bell owners of Har-Bell, Basil and Bonus Frost of Frost Sporting Goods, Jerry and Beverly Burwell of Burr's, Everett and Fern Payne of Magic Country Beef, and Roy and Ila Calfee of Scenic Shoppers and others all of whom financed teams for many years. Without the support of these businesses the city's softball history would have been greatly diminished.

I hope you can enjoy and perhaps relate to this collection of stories.

# ONE

## GRANT BEACH PARK

We sat on the concrete bleachers along the south end of the of the ball field. A low rock wall ran along the right field line and made a 90-degree angle eastward toward centerfield. A high screen protected the short distance from home plate. A large oak tree shaded that end of the bleachers and a small kid's merry-go-round and cooled the breeze from the southwest.

My uncle had told us of the exploits of one of the Triple A league pitchers who threw for A and A Shopette, a small grocery store that sponsored one of the teams. To my dismay the game was early and had already started without him, and going into the second inning it was tied at one run each.

The entrance to the field was a small gate right behind home plate, and I noticed a guy waiting to come in between pitches. Dressed in white shirt, tie, and dark slacks, carrying a pair of spikes, a ball cap, and a glove, he dashed in and went to the bench on the first base side. He quickly stripped off the tie and shirt revealing a white t-shirt, donned his cap and spikes, rolled up his slacks, and drafted one of his teammates who had been lounging on the rock wall smoking a cigarette. Hurriedly warming up, he signaled that he was ready, and the manager walked to the rubber and made the pitching change.

His motion was much different than the usual windmill or occasional slingshot throwers. With elbow out, his hand went in front of his face then twirled around his head into launch position. He threw drop ball after drop ball, sizzling in at the knees and sharply diving down and in, to right-handers. It became quickly apparent that most guys couldn't touch him and the best hitters might hope to hit a high bouncer to the infield.

His name was Gene Barr and just as quickly he became my idol. I later found out he had made his way to Springfield, Missouri, from a small town farther north named Marshall and pitched one year for the Clearwater Bombers, a legendary team from Florida that was a national power and several times national champions. At that time he held the national tournament record for second most innings pitched in a game — 24 2/3 — losing on an error 2-0 while playing for Springfield's Barnes Store team.

Softball was big in Springfield in the fifties and sixties and the Triple A league was the biggest draw. The teams played on Tuesdays at Grant Beach Park and Fridays at Fassnight Park and normally had several hundred spectators in attendance. The second game on Friday was broadcast on the radio and the News and Leader newspaper not only sponsored a team but regularly ran box scores and a once-a-week column devoted to the sport.

With no college baseball teams in the area and a weak semi-pro league, the best place to keep playing were the nearly 200 softball teams. In the fifties many local high schools had softball teams that kept a steady supply of pitchers ready to fill the ranks. The Triple A league was filled with players of top talent, many who had been signed by professional baseball teams and had minor league experience and a few who made it for a brief time to the big leagues.

The pitchers were the stars and dominated play. Good throwers would get 10-15 strikeouts a game. The catchers and first- and third-base players kept the game lively with quick throws to each other between pitches. The infielders on the lines played several steps in front of the bags to prevent or field bunts, which were a big part of the game.

The quickness of the game made it a great spectator sport. Much faster than baseball, with 60-foot baselines, 250-foot fences, and the pitcher only 46 feet away throwing at speeds in the high 80s and 90s and some even over 100 miles per hour, and with games lasting seven innings, it was baseball in double-time. There were also rise balls, drop balls, and change-ups to deal with, and most good pitchers had all three pitches in their repertoire.

I was introduced into this softball community by my uncles, Delbert, or Deke, and Richard, who regularly stopped at our house on game days to pick up my brother Jim, me and any neighborhood kids, like next door friend Steve, we could fit into Deke's '59 Impala. It became a game I loved to watch and participate in and I devoted a good amount of time to learning the game. Most homes did not have air conditioning, and television offered only three stations and no weekday sports. Harry Carey and Jack Buck provided radio coverage of the St. Louis Cardinals baseball team, but if you wanted to stay somewhat cool and watch a game in person you had to head to one of the local parks.

The concrete stands at Grant Beach and Fassnight parks were very close to the field and if you wanted a good view of the pitchers, you chose a seat near the fence. From that vantage point you got a really good feel for the speed and movement of the pitches.

Many top-of-the-line teams played in tournaments and exhibition games in Springfield and brought with them elite pitchers from the Midwest. Jerry Ralfs from Cedar Rapids, Iowa, Harlan Schlesener, Don and Darrell Rosenow from Kansas, Dub Lowery and Ed Boncek of St. Louis, Jack Burkhart from Kansas City, Bill Massey and Sam Beavers from Texas, Daryl Flint from St. Joseph, and Harvey Sterkel and Charlie Richard of the Aurora SealMasters (several time national champions) all had my complete attention from right behind the plate.

1968 World Champion Aurora Sealmasters

Front row: George Giles, Ray Phillips, Dave Timok, Manager Smith, Don Voigt, Marv Detloff, Happy Cox

Back row: Fred Blum, Steve Neilson, Harvey Sterkel, Ed Greer, Billy Stewart, Charlie Richard, George Kinder, Bob Christensen, Frank Hurt, Joe Lynch, Larry Wiseman, Commissioner Jensen

Of that group Bill Massey was the most impressive. At about 6'4" he was tall and rangy with long arms and huge hands. It seemed I could see the air currents flowing off the seams of that reverse rotation as the ball rose from the batter's waist to his shoulders at over 90 miles an hour. Bill didn't lose a lot of games.

However, in my opinion, the best pitcher I ever saw was Joe Lynch from the Aurora, Illinois, team. They played two exhibition games in Springfield and he pitched a no-hitter that night against a very talented Barnes Store team. That wasn't unusual since he had rolled into town that year with an undefeated record for the summer. Big and burly he possessed a good drop ball but his rise ball was his calling card. I sat almost directly behind the plate and from there it appeared as though he threw the ball directly down at the ground and about halfway to the hitter it began a sharp rise over any swinging bats. Bob McLish was a national tournament MVP one year and said that he had batted five times against Joe

Island, New York.

Most of the News and Leader team worked in their circulation department. A large paper route at that time might have several hundred deliveries per day and could bring in a good salary. Others might work in the mail room, on the docks, or restocking the vending machines around town.

The champion caliber Aurora, Illinois team employed players who incorporated softball practice as part of their day on a softball field at the bearings plant. Many players were coaches and teachers in the area, which allowed them more freedom to play and travel during the summer.

The Frisco railroad line was a big employer in town and the company held its own tournament during the fifties. One of the teams came from Memphis and featured flame thrower "Buck" Miller. Ancil Fry batted against him early in Ancil's career and he stated that the ball looked like an aspirin tablet crossing the plate.

Uniforms copied Major League Baseball styles of the day, and following the Pirates win over the Yankees in 1960 the Foremost Dairy team paraded out white sleeveless uniforms with blue stripes down the legs and blue sleeved undershirts. The Barnes Store teams for years wore Milwaukee Braves uniforms with Barnes emblazoned across the front. The well-financed teams of the era provided their players with high school letterman style warm-up jackets. They were ridiculously hot during the summer months but looked awesome. Pitchers always wore them but usually just inserted the throwing arm while on the bench between innings.

The hot stove league, which was any assemblage of fast pitch aficionados, ran rampant during the winter months with lots of speculation among players and fans on how the players might realign going into the season. The AAA level in Springfield was a pretty exclusive society and unless you knew someone or were a player of note it was hard to break into the circle. Although the games were very competitive and sometimes vindictive there was always a level of camaraderie and respect for the other team's talent.

This was not your recreational softball league where players showed up only when they wanted or didn't work to improve their skills. The good players were well known around town and possessed a level of swagger knowing they were the best of the best. To be a member of a state or regional champion greatly enhanced your reputation, and a trip to the nationals really raised your standing in the softball community.

Every team entered the new season with high expectations especially if they had made some improvements to their roster. A highly regarded pitcher could mean a swing of several games in the league and boosted your chances in district or state competition. Depending on the year, three or four teams from Springfield would qualify for the state tournament. The championship revolved from St. Joseph to Jefferson City and then back to Springfield. The number of teams registered in each district determined how many teams could qualify from that area. Springfield and St. Joseph always had the most teams, with Joplin and Jefferson City usually sending two each.

Kansas City and St. Louis held metro tournaments with the winner in each city moving on to the Regional. At that time the Midwest Regional consisted of four state champions, Kansas, Nebraska, Iowa and Missouri, with a host team from the city where the tournament was to be played joining the Omaha, Kansas City and St. Louis metro winners and the defending champion. So, if a city team won the state, another served as host team, and it had the winner from last year's regional. It could possibly have three teams in the nine-team tournament.

Opening nights at the state or regional regularly drew crowds of 1,500 to 2,000 for each session to marvel at the teams and especially the pitchers. Springfield played host to several state tournaments and were always fun to watch. Besides seeing great players from St. Joseph, Jefferson City and Cape Girardeau, there were also subpar teams from around the state. One player from a small town carried a glove with no stringing. We were sitting in the Fassnight bleachers and Virgil Fredrick, taking notice, stated, "That glove went for five dollars down, no strings attached." Upon hearing one player in the loser's bracket at Doling Park complaining about the condition of the field Robert Rice simply stated in a loud voice, "You play where your ability dictates."

Cape sent good squads to the tournament featuring pitchers Gil Roberts and John Watkins. Watkins was also one of the better hitters in Missouri and he along with shortstop Lindon "Meat"

Duncan and catcher/first baseman Bill Parker were great to watch. Those teams were champions in 1957, 1958, 1960, 1961 and 1967. Starting in 1935 St. Joe teams won 10 of 11 state events, and Springfield followed suit between 1946 and 1956 with the same run. Teams from St. Joseph took top honors in 1962, 1963 and 1965 with stalwarts Bill McKinney and Daryl Flint on the mound and backed by hitters like Dave Dewey, Duane Groenke and Roger Shephard. Flint had been a star basketball player at Maryville State College. He had a thick shock of black hair and wore his cap cocked on the back of his head earning him the dubious title of "Pretty Boy" from Springfield fans.

Springfield entertained regional championships in 1958, 1959, 1960, 1963 and 1966. This tournament was a step up in the pitching department. St. Louis had throwers Ed Boncek, Ralph Baker, Howie Lamb and Charley "Dub" Lowery. Souix City, Iowa, featured Springfieldian Tim Buff in 1958. He pitched for Des Moines in 1966 and brought slugger Bob McLish back with him when he returned home.

Springfield teams could throw pitchers like Roy Grantham, Gene Barr, Allen McCann, Artie Charle, Earl Rivers, Larry Marshall and Larry Atwood into the fray. Kansas consistently featured the Rosenow brothers and Harlan (Charlie) Schlesener. Charlie was a Kansas wheat farmer and a renowned hurler. He generally threw for teams from Wichita but usually ended up in the regional since the state winner wisely used him as a pickup player. Legend has it that the lanky right hander always brought a sleeping cot and a pint of whisky with him to the ballpark. Between games he would stretch out on the cot and enjoy a few sips but he was always ready for the next game. One year Foremost Dairy sent him a letter offering him a job at the dairy if he would move to Springfield and pitch for them. He replied that he really wasn't looking for a job but might be interested in buying the dairy. I believe that pretty much ended negotiations.

I loved opening night.

# THREE

## THE BRAMER LEGACY

The earliest and perhaps the most influential manager in Springfield's rise to importance at the state, regional, and national level was Ed Bramer. Ed played with Holy Name in the 1930's and the St. Joseph Church team in Springfield in the early forties. In 1946 he organized and managed the Knights of Columbus team which became the first Springfield team to win the Missouri state tournament and followed up that same season with a first regional crown and trip to the World Tournament. It was the first year the state had been played outside of St. Joseph, Missouri. Teams from St. Joseph had dominated state play since its inception in 1934 winning ten of the twelve tournaments. Ed Bramer had a great understanding of how the game should and would be played. Besides recognizing talent and team chemistry his savvy in using the bunt and base stealing to maximize his team's abilities revolutionized the game in Springfield. His tactics helped overcome teams with better talent. His methods prevailed for several decades being copied to some extent by later successful managers Larry Atwood, Guy McConnell, Jim Little and Jim Horton. Ed Bramer's clubs would become the standard of success for the next 15 years.

Following the end of World War II a flood of soldiers returned to the United States. Many of them had learned to love the game of softball during their deployment. Bramer stocked his team with several of those men including a few who had played professional baseball before going to serve their country. The core of Bramer's team included Larue Savage, Paul Smith, Floyd (Froggy) McDaniel, Max McCandless, Charles Tally, Ed Lechner, Jack Horton, David Martin, Greg Ricketts, and Bus Harless. The pitching staff on the original Knights of Columbus included Hugh Ricketts, Leo Augustine, Larry smith and Tom Doyle. Doyle had been a well- advised pickup after the district and proven his worth in tournament play.

The Bramer team would go on to win the next three state tournaments under different sponsorships. The 1947 and 1948 teams played under the banner of White Front Caseys and the 1949 team represented Ford Tractors. The 1947 and 1949 teams went on to finish second in regional tournaments held in St. Joe. The power packed 1948 Caseys team would win the regional and make a run at a World Tournament title before finishing fourth in Portland, Oregon. Big Tom Doyle was impressive in the state tournament in Springfield hurling three no-hitters in the team's run to victory. Springfield was a desired destination for the meet because of the crowds of people drawn to the park. The 1948 tournament saw 2500 fans on hand for the finals held at Fassnight Park. Springfield had become a cash cow for the ASA and the tournament was on exhibit in Springfield for several years in a row.

Tom Doyle

The 1950 Ford Tractors team was defeated in the winners' bracket finals by eventual champion Jefferson City Larry's Tavern and pitching showman "Mousey" Mathis finishing in third-place. The 1951 squad showcasing a pitching staff of Doyle, Glen Bell and Gene Smith were upset in the district but the Springfield district winner Coca-Cola with John Higgens and Don Iseminger toeing the slab advanced on to win the state. The team now playing as the Colonials had received a bid to play in the ASA outlawed league NSA's national tournament in Phoenix, Arizona and they accepted at some expense. Although winning their seventh straight league and city championships in 1952 the Colonials were suspended from participation in any ASA tournaments including the district and state. Once again, a Springfield team was triumphant at the state meet when Patton Tastemark led by pitchers Artie Charlie and Bill Darnell took the Missouri State Championship.

The Bramer team was at it again in 1953 appearing as Peer Hardware and took back the state championship while qualifying for the regional tournament. The addition of stalwart pitcher Lefty Vickers from Cape Giraudeau, Missouri had made the mound core even stronger. The Peer Hardware squad followed up that crown with another in 1954 and a runner up finish in the Omaha, Nebraska regional thanks to a great pitching staff of Glen Bell, Ron Iseminger, and Artie Charle. Bramer switched sponsors again in 1955 but it didn't change the outcome as his News and Leader club took state honors and again finished second in regional play, for the first time held in Springfield. It was the seventh state tournament title for Bramer in 10 years of play.

In 1956 with sponsor Barnes Store now emblazoned across their shirts the Bramer managed team again won league and city titles but instead of playing in the district they choose again to accept a bid to the National Softball League's national meet held in New Bedford, Illinois. The players had now all learned to use an alias at the outlawed tournament. The Barnes team duplicated their league and city exploits in 1957 but the ASA found a way to punish them by suspending Jerry Gregg, Glen Bell, Bob Allen, and J.C. Loveland. That took the entire pitching staff and later former minor leaguer Bud Routh was suspended to insure they would not have enough players to compete in the playoff game against

Tastemark to earn the regional host team spot. Ironically Ed Bramer was now managing the Tastemark team and he was banned from participating in the regional as well. His Tastemark team went on to play in that tournament and take second to defending champion News and Leader.

Bramer placed his team again under the Tastemark emblem in 1958 and by virtue of their ninth straight league and city title qualified to serve as the 1958 Western Regional host team to be played in Springfield. That championship was won by St. Louis Thurmer's. The 1959 Tastemark team won the state tournament but didn't make it out of the regional won by Springfield's Barnes Store team as they advanced to the National Tournament. The 1960 Tastemark team was Bramer's last. That team managed a third-place finish in state tournament play.

In addition to his success as a manager of men's teams Bramer also coached some very talented women's clubs. His Central Labor Union team took second in 1953 and 1954 and then won two state championships in 1955 and 1956. Under the sponsorship of Barnes Store his teams won titles in 1957, 1958, and 1959 giving them a string of five straight titles. His last year of coaching in 1960 only managed a second-place state tournament finish losing to another Springfield team the Knockers featuring top pitcher and hitter Kay Hunter.

In a career spanning 15 years Ed Bramer's men's teams had won 12 Springfield league titles and advanced to state tournament competition 13 times and won eight times. They had participated in 10 regional championships, winning two, and four world meets. His women's teams had garnered five championships and played in eight straight state tournament finals and qualified for five regionals. All together his clubs amassed 13 state tournament crowns, participated in 21 of them, played in 15 regionals with two championships, and took four trips to world tournaments. A pretty good legacy.

# Four

## Barnes Store

Clell Barnes was the owner of Barnes General Store, mostly a furniture store that served western Springfield, and beginning in the early 1950s sponsor of Barnes Store. A team that was dominant in the '60s after earning a host spot in the 1959 regional held in Springfield. Springfield Tastemark had won the state tournament behind the pitching of Arte Charle and Earl Rivers. St. Louis Thurmer's was the defending champion and featured hurlers Bob Allen and Ralph Baker and a squad of great hitters. Barnes was an extremely young team and had won the league with pitchers Roy Grantham and manager Larry Atwood.

At age 22, Atwood had assembled a squad of mostly fraternity brothers from Southwest Missouri State University that embodied great defense and timely hitting. The core of that team held together for most of the decade. Third baseman Sammy Potter and second sacker Jay Kinser were loyal for the entire time, and key players Bonus Frost, Oliver Smith, Jr. Williams, Jim Little, Danny Walsworth, Bob "Speedy" Cobb, Bud Routh, Jerry Bernet, Dan Bishop and Bill Ruyle were pretty consistent team members.

With the additions of pickup players Barr and Cape Girardeau's John Watkins, Barnes won the regional and qualified for the

National Tournament when Barr bested former Springfieldian Bob Allen pitching for St. Louis in the finals. Barnes remained a force in the AAA league, winning several titles, and reemerged in the national spotlight in 1966 winning as regional host and playing in the nationals in Indianapolis, Indiana, and represented Springfield when the city entertained its first national tournament as host team in the 1967 national tournament won by the Aurora, Illinois, Sealmasters.

As a pitcher Larry Atwood was not overwhelming but all of his pitches moved and he possessed pinpoint control. He knew how to pitch to every hitter in the league which made him dominant in everyday play. As a manager he stressed fundamentals and the importance of advancing runners into scoring position. The Barnes team seemed always capable of scoring a few runs and manufacturing them in key situations. In a game based on pitching a couple of runs went a long way. Barnes Store remained the team to beat until the sponsorship ended after the 1969 season with the team winning its first and last state championship and playing in the regional for the last time.

Big left-handed pitcher Roy Grantham was a tough pitcher and a power hitter. He provided excellent pitching in clutch games for Barnes in state and regional play. His good control and big-breaking pitchers made it difficult to make good contact from even the best of hitters. Artie Charle and Gene Smith provided good mound work later in the decade. Phil Wilkerson was the main hurler for the 1969 champions.

In tournament play teams were usually allotted time for infield practice and by far the most impressive was the Barnes Store team. I remember the excitement of watching their fielders picking up ground balls and whipping them around the diamond from player to player with seemingly each throw arriving chest high and then zipping to the next position. I had my eyes opened to what having a good arm meant when watching Ollie Smith firing the ball in from center field with every throw coming in very fast and ending up over third base right at third baseman Sammy Potter's knees. It was just a calling card to the opposing team reminding them not to try for an extra base on a base hit or fly ball to center.

Barnes' run production method was simple and effective. Second baseman Jay Kinser was very adept at getting on base whether through being hit, walking, by error, or an occasional base hit. He was usually advanced by Sammy Potter who had excellent bat control. He could bunt for a sacrifice, cover for a steal attempt, or hit the ball to the opposite side of the infield in a hit and run. When third-place hitter Bonus Frost came to the plate Kinser was usually in scoring position at second base or, even better, safely at third. Bonus almost annually led the AAA league in hitting. He had some power but was a contact hitter who sprayed hits all over the diamond. Add to that the fact that he was also very fast and always added a lot of leg hits to his batting average.

This plan seemed to work one or two times a game and any runs added by the rest of the team just added to the difficulty of beating them. The team used their speed to put pressure on the other team's defense and it proved to be a valuable asset to their winning ways. In the decade between 1959 and 1969 Barnes played in four regional tournaments, winning two, and participated in three national tournaments. The team provided a good road map for later teams to follow as an example of how the game should be played for success.

Barnes General Store:

In front-Batboy Tommy Smith

Front row: Bill Knight, Bill Manary, Gene Smith, Sam Potter, Junior Williams, Jay Kinser, Mort Edwards

Back row: Clell Barnes, Larry Atwood, Artie Charlie, Bonus Frost, Danny Bishop, Steve Hutchinson, Wayne McKinney, Tom Majors, Bud Routh

# Five

## News and Leader

The News and Leader Parrots were the kings of Springfield and Missouri state softball in the mid to late 1950s. They won state tournaments in 1955 and 1956, and appeared in four straight regional tournaments and became champions in 1956 and 1957. They played in national championships those two years, one in Clearwater, Florida, and the other at Sacramento, California, where they finished fourth.

The mainstay on the mound was left hander Roy Grantham along with Glenn "Dinger" Bell, Jim "Lefty" Vickers, Bob Glover and a pair of talented teenaged pitchers, Allen McCann and Larry Marshall. Marshall won the 1957 regional finals in relief at the age of 18. Gene Barr added pitching support in 1958 with Larry Atwood joining as a pickup after state competition.

The basis of those clubs included steady hitting second baseman Bill Manary, power hitters Leon Bischoff and Tom Majors, catcher Denny "Duke" Henry, outfielders Bob Burgess, Bill Knight, line drive smashing LaRue Savage, Bus Harless and Bill Harding, along with infielders Bob "Speedy" Cobb, Larry Smith, Max McCandless and Bob Fender, to name a few.

The newspaper ended its sponsorship for several years before building powerful teams in the mid-1960s until the mid-1970s.

Harold Wreche was not only the Parrots manager he was also circulation manager for Springfield Newspapers. He rebuilt the newspaper team starting in 1963 by establishing a core of players whom he had hired on to work there. Ronnie and Stan Shank worked there along with Leon Bischoff, Buddy Foell, Ted West, Tim Buff, Denver Dixon, Bob McLish, Wayne Ryan and Gene Barr, among many others. The Parrots of the late '60s and early '70s were usually based on strong pitching and a power hitting lineup. The team always had plenty of punch up and down the lineup with almost all of them supplying home run potential.

Allen McCann anchored the pitching corps in the late '50's and early '60s with a powerful rise ball and lots of zip. His telephone company job caused him to move to Flat River, Missouri, where he pitched a team into the '66 and '67 state tournaments. He also played in the 1968 championship with St. Joe Walnut Products. Wreche had lured big time thrower Tim Buff back to hometown Springfield after a year toiling for Des Moines, Iowa, and pitching them to a regional berth in 1966. Des Moines's top hitter, Bob McLish, was enticed to join him in Springfield as well. Steady players Phil Groover, Dub Ward, John Bailey, Jim Cotner, Max Miller and Neill Smith all spent time playing for the newspaper team, as well as riseballer Kenny Williams.

One night the umpire wouldn't give Kenny the ball he wanted to throw so on the next pitch he tossed it over the Fassnight screen and out of the park. I remember Dub Ward arguing a called strike with one of the umpires and then hitting the next pitch over the high right field screen at Grant Beach Park. As he touched home plate he made another remark to the ump and was immediately ejected from the game.

Neill Smith wasn't a great defensive outfielder and thus he was nicknamed "Colonel Clink". It was rumored he had bought his ball glove from a local metal salvage. He, however, was very capable of launching towering shots over the right field wall. Denver Dixon began playing for the newspaper out of high school in 1964 and became known for both his hitting and infielding skills. Denver could play almost every position and spent time with the Clearwater Bombers and later a national contending Cedar Rapids, Iowa, team. Jim Maggi, Donnie Haworth and Don Marrs all played several years with the Parrots. Always anchored in the middle of the lineup was line drive hitter Ronnie Crosswhite. Usually slotted into the cleanup position, he protected some of the best hitters ever to play in Springfield by being a fierce competitor with the bat and a tough out with runners in scoring position.

It was normal procedure for each team playing a game to contribute two new softballs at the start of the game. Squaring off one day at the Joplin Tri-State Tournament was manager Jim Little's Scenic Shopper nine and the Parrots. After a few foul balls were hit out of play and long home runs by Stan Shank and Don Marrs, steaming pitcher R.C. Crowe was looking for a ball to continue play. Approaching the plate from the on-deck circle Crosswhite teased R.C. "You're going to have to wait a while, Little had to go back to Springfield for more balls." Not amused, Crowe sent the first pitch near Ronnie's head. Picking himself off the ground Crosswhite headed to the mound, but cooler heads prevailed and order was restored.

The newspaper fielded a really good ball club in 1971, winning the state title in Springfield over Jefferson City Rippeto Carpet and thrower John Watkins. Phil Wilkerson was a tough pitcher but was also a good hitter. In the last inning the Parrots were down 1-0 and had a man on base but were down to their last out. Wilkerson was called on to pinch hit and he hammered a home run over the left field wall giving the team a win and a state title. Someone on the newspaper team joked that Phil was the only one goofy enough to pull that off. That murderer's row of hitters included Jim Maggi, Jim Smith, Don Marrs, Ronnie Crosswhite, Wayne Ryan, Denver Dixon, Stan Shank, Phil Groover, Tom Majors, and manager Sam Potter.

I was privileged to give up 12 runs and as many hits to the Parrots in two innings one August night at Grant Beach. The only positive outcome for me was that no one hit one out of the park.

The team played in the regional tournament losing in the finals to Cedar Rapids, Iowa, and renowned pitcher Jerry Ralfs. The Iowa squad went on to win the National title, also held in Springfield. The Parrots finished strong in state play through 1976 finishing in the top three several times and second the last year. The Newspaper provided good paying jobs for lots of players and a lot of thrills for Springfield fans over three decades.

# SIX

## TWO DAIRIES AND A BANK

Tastemark/Foremost Dairy sponsored top rate softball teams from the '40s until the late '70s. They built powerhouse teams winning the state tournament in 1952, 1959 and 1966 and finishing second in two more championships. They were regional qualifiers in 1957 as well finishing second to a great Springfield News and Leader team. Mainstays for those early teams were rise ball pitcher Artie Charle and hurlers Bob Allen and Gene Smith. The team included infielders Max Miller, Larry Smith, Gene Smith, Larry Giboney, Jerry Gregg and Ancil Fry. Ron Walsworth and Joe Hasten usually handled the catching duties, with Tom Majors, Bill Ruyle and Danny Clopton patrolling the outfield.

The sponsor named changed from Tastemark to Foremost in 1962 and brought together one of the best hitting teams, in my opinion, to ever play in Springfield. Bob Speake had played outfield with Chicago Cubs and San Francisco Giants for a couple of years and joined hitters like Jack Hasten, Bonus Frost, Ollie Smith, Leon Bischoff, Max Miller, Bob Price and Ancil Fry to make a formable line-up. Add to that mix throwers Tim Buff, Allen McCann and lefty Earl Rivers and you had the makings of a great team. The team finished as state runner up in that year and was in contention for the next six years, winning it all in 1966 with Gene Barr and R.C. Crowe providing most of the pitching. The '66 team took third-place in the regional tournament held in Springfield that year.

The 1968 team was another of my favorites. The squad lost their state tournament opening night game by one run to Jefferson City and pitcher Mousey Mathis. They bounced back to win nine games in a row in the loser's bracket over two days before losing to Barnes Store in the bracket finals finishing in third-place. The state team had awesome pitching with Gene Barr, Kenny Williams and Phil Wilkerson. We watched a late-night game played at Westport Park where the lighting was dim at best especially after a fairly dense fog rolled in. Hard throwing Wilkerson was on the mound and was literally unhittable in the darkness. It was difficult in the dimness to see centerfielder Tom Majors in position in the outfield and even harder for the Joplin hitters to see Phil's 90-miles-an-hour rise ball. The club consisted of Mike Greene at first base, Jack Hasten at second, Denver Dixon at shortstop, Ancil Fry played third, Jim McDaniel, Ron Shank, Tom Majors and Don Marrs covered the outfield, while Majors and Joe Marler did the catching. Jerry Gregg was a valuable utility man being a solid hitter and versatile defensive player.

Manager/third sacker Ancil Fry reassembled a team of unlikely heroes to form a really good hitting team in 1973. A mixture of veterans such as Leon Bischoff, Fry, and Jim McDaniel blended in with slick fielding Steve Hutton at short, defensive ace catcher Mark Gann, and hurler Gene Barr to form a solid nucleus. The Johnson brothers, Gary and Rick, John Ryan and newcomers Mike McTeer and Charlie Essary rounded out the team. The team went on a hitting frenzy in the second half of the year tying Scenic for the league lead before losing to that club 4-3 when Bob McLish lashed a three-run homer late in the contest.

Under the names of A and A Shopette and Cloverleaf Dairy and Adams Milk, one of Springfield's most successful squads took shape. Starting in 1960 and ending after the 1964 season the team played in four regional tournaments, winning two of those, and participated strongly in two national championships. The '60 team was solid with players John Gardner, Bud Routh, Tom Majors,

Buddy Foell, Leon Bischoff, J.C. Loveland, Bill Manary, Jerry Gregg, Speedy Cobb and Gene Smith. The pitching staff included pick up player Larry Marshall, Glenn Bell and Gene Barr. The team ran into national powerhouses Clearwater, Florida, and Aurora, Illinois, falling to the Bombers in 15 innings and losing to Harvey Sterkel and the Sealmasters 1-0.

When Barr hit the road to pitch for Clearwater in 1961 Bob Allen was enticed back home after pitching for St. Louis Thurmer's Bar for two years. A and A added steady infielder Shorty Harrison and good hitting Bob Price to the lineup as they attempted to defend their regional title only to lose to Thurmer's in St. Louis. A rebuilt team hosted and won the 1963 regional as Barr rejoined the club and drop baller Tim Buff was picked up. The duo combined great pitching allowing only one run in the dash to the championship. The team returned to St. Louis in 1964 again as defending champs. Those teams were made up of Mike Greene, Larry Hale, Bill Manary, Ken Williams, Jim Rader, Billy Bain, Bob Turner, Gene Smith, Shorty Harrison and Gene Cunningham. Big hitters Jack Hasten and Bob Price were added as pick-up players from the Foremost squad. They provided timely hits with Price delivering a grand slam homer in the final game of the '63 tournament.

A young, fast, intensely aggressive team sponsored by Empire Bank changed the landscape for the AAA league starting in 1963 and continuing through 1969. Formed by player/manager Guy McConnell, the club possessed speed, power and good defense to back their hustle and pressure. Mild mannered Jim Maggi was a clothing salesman by day and an ever-churning composite of arms and legs when he took to the field. A free-swinging batter, he got more hits off of balls out of the strike zone than anyone of the day. Fast on the bases Maggi was always pushing for that extra base causing lots of problems for the opponent's defenders. Centerfielder Ron Sharpe added speed and good defense while Wayne Ferry, Ronnie Crosswhite and Larry Taunt provided power in the middle of the lineup. Steady players Donnie Haworth, Craig Soltys, Terry Snider, and catcher Ted West added to the mix. Shelby Hill and Glenn Bell did the mound work. The team ran their way to a state title in 1964 and played in the regional that year. They finished second in the 1966 state losing to a good

Springfield Foremost team in the finals. By 1969 the bank had lured great hitter Don Marrs, first baseman Jim Smith, and outfielder Jim McDaniel to the team and added Dick Davis and Tom Osborne. Big "Black Jack" Kassonivoid from Oklahoma was the mainstay on the mound with support from Hill, Bell, Gary McDaniel and Jim Shaw. The bank ceased its sponsorship after the team served as host team for the 1969 National Tournament.

Sponsored by Empire Bank

Front row: Terry Snider, Wayne Ferry, Donnie Haworth, Jim Maggi, Winston Ackerman, Jim Smith, Shelby Hill, Dickie Davis

Back Row: Speedy Cobb, Larry Taunt, Bob Price, "Black Jack" Kassanavoid, Jim McDaniel, Don Marrs, Gary McDaniel, Tom Osbern, Glenn Bell, Keith Davis

# SEVEN

## ICONS

There were lots of good hitters in the '60's but in my mind the purest power hitter was Jack Hasten. From the bleachers he seemed almost larger than life with strong forearms and large powerful hands. When he took his stance and dug in you could almost see the sawdust falling from the bat grip as he wrapped his fingers around it. Jack had played for several years in the Philadelphia Phillies organization moving up to the AAA team. The thing about Jack was that he had much less than average speed and an average arm, two barriers that probably kept him at the minor league level. He could hit for average while drilling line drives all over the park, with lots of them clearing the fence. Jack was a clutch hitter, winning many games at every level getting timely hits with men in scoring positions. One night a group of my friends and I were out fooling around and we ended up at the batting cages at a miniature golf course. To our enjoyment Jack was there putting on a hitting display and complaining that the machine didn't throw hard enough. We talked briefly and I was telling him how I was thinking about not pitching anymore due a very humiliating loss in the league the night before. Jack laughed and said, "They can beat ya but they can't eat ya. You can always come back tomorrow." I followed his advice.

Among other hitters of note was Leon Bishoff. A catcher and a first baseman, he was a great batter for two decades. He had been retired from the sport for a few years but was talked back into playing by Foremost's Ancil Fry. Although the overall pitching level was probably weaker, Leon, at the age of 42, batted over .400 for the year. One night I saw Bill Shepard hit two towering home runs off Gene Barr seemingly carrying to the pool down the right field line at Fassnight park. It was one of the few times I saw Barr give up a home run and the only time I ever saw anyone hit two off of him. Ronnie Crosswhite came into the league early in the decade and was consistently a vital cog in the middle of all of his teams' lineups. Don Marrs and Jim McDaniel came on later after both had played minor league baseball in the Kansas City Athletics' system. Marrs set a AAA league record in 1969, hitting over .500 for the year and hitting seven home runs in league play. Jim McDaniel was an excellent outfielder and combined power and average for several years. Bob McLish was voted the most valuable hitter in the 1973 National Tournament, setting a championship record with five home runs. When Hasten had learned that McLish was the tournament MVH he noted, "Nothing against Bobby, but if he did that well I would have hit a ton!" During a state tournament game Wayne "Doc" Miller had backed Bob off the plate with a head high rise ball. The next pitch was driven over the right field fence and McLish loudly cussed Miller all the way around the bases calling him a squirrel doctor among many other things. "Doc" was a veterinarian.

Through the decade the same players could be counted on to be in the top ten list of batting averages. Gene Smith, small and wiry, time after time delivered offerings from top pitchers on a line to the outfield playing for Adams Dairy and Barnes Store. Empire Bank's Jim Maggi would swing at and hit almost every pitch delivered to him. I sat in amazement one evening as he hit a pitch in the dirt on the first bounce up the middle for a clean single. Versatile Junior Williams could play almost every position in the field and combined some power with his speed to be a steady .300 hitter. Larry Hale was considered the fastest player in the league and would constantly post high numbers in batting average and runs scored from his lead off position. Larry told me it took him nine steps to get to the bag after he hit the ball which didn't leave much time for an infielder to throw to first base.

Year after year, however, the hardest player to keep off the bases was Bonus Frost. Bonus had power, a great eye, and hit the pitch wherever it was thrown using all fields. His upper body and arms hung out over the plate from the left side taking away almost half of the strike zone. To Bonus a hit batsman was as good as a base hit in a game with few run scoring opportunities. In one plate appearance during a district tournament game lefty Earl Rivers hit him three times, but the umpire ruled he had not tried to get out of the way. It didn't bother Bonus to get hit and it didn't bother Earl to hit him. Stalemate.

As much as I idolized the big hitters, the stars of the show were the pitchers. Some of them were better than most of the others but each of them was really good, and I dreamed of joining their ranks. I imagined how great it would feel to be on the rubber with the game on the line and all eyes on you as you blew away the competition. Larry Atwood of Barnes Store owned the league with his pin point control and knowledge of every hitter. From the district level up to the nationals, Gene Barr was the best Springfield could offer and repeatedly starred in tournament play. Long and lanky Tim Buff threw effortlessly with a big breaking drop ball and an occasional curve ball that seemed to move three feet. He was probably the best fielding pitcher I remember and he could throw over handed to the bases, which seems simple, but lots of good throwers never seemed to get the hang of it. Kenny Williams came from Texas via St. Joseph and brought with him a devastating rise ball. I learned how to throw a rise watching Kenny game after game. With his forefinger bent and pushing against a seam he stepped slightly toward third base allowing him to throw across his body. That move enabled him to get his hand under the ball better and kept it hid from the batter's eye just a second longer as it seemed to get on the hitter much faster. I don't remember Kenny ever throwing a game when his rise ball wasn't working. Drop ball artist Larry Marshall and flame thrower Allen McCann were mainstays for News and Leader teams through the mid '60s. Burly Shelby "Moose" Hill anchored the Empire bank staff for several years, teaming with Glenn Bell and Roy Grantham to win a state championship. Scenic Shopper teams in the late '60s featured hurlers R.C. Crowe and Jim Collins. Gary McDaniel began his career during that time and, although not a world beater, probably had more wins than any pitcher in AAA history. This was the fraternity I longed to belong to, with throwing arm thrust into a warm up jacket and sporting a toe plate on one shoe and, hopefully, at least one fan impressed with it all.

# Eight

## Early On

The concrete bleachers became steadily more uncomfortable as the evening wore on. Regular fans often brought pillows or cushions to soften the hardness of the stands or left after a game or two, but diehards like Uncles Deke and Richard and brother Jim, Steve Hutsell, Robert Rice and I were there for the duration. A trip to the concession stand for a Coke and a Zero candy bar offered some relief and the cool of the summer evening made the role of spectator bearable. I can vividly remember the scrape and scuffle of spikes on the concrete walkways marking the changing of teams between games and the metamorphosing of work-a-day men into twice-a-week heroes on the field.

The mid 1960s to 1972 was, to me, the best overall that Springfield softball had to offer. With five quality teams in the league and usually a couple more competitive squads, Springfield dominated state play, winning seven of nine state championships. Jim Little's Scenic Shopper teams won three of those tournaments while Empire Bank, News and Leader, Barnes Store, and Foremost all won one. Long-time pitching nemeses Daryl Flint of St. Joseph and John Watkins playing for New Hamburg took championships in 1965 and 1967 respectively. Flint pitched and won all six games for the St. Joseph Athletes for their win. During that time St. Louis Deville, basically the old Thurmer's Bar team, won regionals in 1964 and 1965 and took second in 1966. Deville boasted hitters Charley Miller and Kenny Heck to go along with the great pitching of Howie Lamb and Dub Lowery. Wichita came to the fore in 1967 and 1968 behind throwers Charlie Shlesener, Charlie Rappard and Billy Ray Jackson.

My introduction into competitive softball started during those years. After several summers of talking brother Jim into catching me in the backyard after supper almost every night I had figured out how to get different spins on the ball to make it move and had developed some zip in my tosses. The bowing out of the chain link fence next to the alley attested to my lack of control, which did improve over time. My Uncle Richard knew of a AA team that had lost its pitcher in the middle of the year in '67 so I eagerly agreed to a short "try out".

My last attempt at making a team had been my freshman year of high school hoping to pitch for the Hillcrest legion baseball team. That had resulted in the long walk of shame home when I was cut. With tears welling up in my eyes and resentment that the coach obviously hadn't recognized my vast amount of talent, I dejectedly made my way back to the house to never throw another baseball. My short tryout with Mono Manufacturing consisted of throwing a few pitches to the catcher and being told I was pitching that night. I threw the last several games for them in the league without a win, but the team wasn't very good. It turned out to be a good learning experience for me realizing I could throw the ball over the plate when I needed to and had some "stuff" as far as repertoire was concerned. I learned I could compete against good hitters in that league like Larry Kellogg, Ernie Meador and Jerry Tillery. One game was lost when the first baseman dropped a throw allowing the winning run to score. After the game he offered his condolences by saying, "Nice game, Big Don. Too bad you had to lose on my error." Amazingly, after several ball games he still didn't know my name.

In 1968 I became involved with a really good Young Men's league sponsored by Midwest Walnut Log Company. Good friend Mike Cluck had been called by up-and-coming AAA pitcher Eddie Brooks to get some guys together to play a practice game against the young team. Mike came by the house and we gathered up our bats and gloves to play the game at Reed Junior High School. I threw well against them and after the game I was invited to join the team. My mom worked in a garment factory that had no air conditioning and air laden with lint particles from the nearly one hundred sewing machines that seemed to whirr and rattle endlessly. Every evening she came home, fashioned a complete meal from scratch and washed the dishes. Once a week she drove me to softball practice at Robberson Elementary and waited patiently in the car, relaxing with a cigarette, until we were finished. We had good players with lots of softball experience. Terry Bowler was a solid catcher, and Richard Wingo was the other pitcher. Bill Fischer played short with a great arm and even greater speed on the bases. The Jones brothers, Joey and Danny, could both hit and both played multiple positions. Darrell Sharick, Terry Scroggins, Randy Keane, Stan Bumgarner, Howard Trent, Fred Anderson and "Boots" Brooks all contributed. The team was managed by Jack Bench and Paul "Rev" Towe. Rod Towe was our best player but we lost him for most of the season due to a broken arm. However, his contribution continued when he recruited fellow Nixa baseball team members Allen Conn and Larry Mathews to play in the league championship game. We trailed First Baptist Church early in that game but we battered pitcher A.B. Blaylock for several runs and I relieved starter Richard Wingo for the win.

    The 1969 season saw Cluck put together a AA league club with me, Jim, Hutsell, Rice, and himself as the nucleus. We worked together to find individual sponsors for each player and called ourselves The Businessmen. Mike was a starting offensive lineman for the Southwest Missouri State Bears and was an agile 260 pounds. Cluck had been enamored with the New York Jets and quarterback Joe Namath, so our only claim to fame was our green and white uniforms and the first white cleats to be worn in the annals of Springfield softball. He managed the team and collected several really good athletes from the football team and former Hillcrest baseball players. The problem was that most had never even seen a fastpitch softball game much less competed against higher level pitching. After a few games against hurlers like Larry Marshall, John Pryor, Jack Dennis, Bucky Price, Leroy Swadley, Al Hanson and Bruce Holloway, several players decided to turn in their uniforms. Joey Jones, Greg Walton, SMS footballer Stan Rinker, roundballer David Richards, and outstanding Parkview High School and Drury College basketball star Virgle Fredrick all stuck it out through the year. A few of us happened to meet up in front of the SMS college union the next fall and Rinker noticed. "Hey, we have all five returning lettermen here."

The best team in the league was Hiland Dairy. Good hitters Jim March, Kent McDaniel, Pat Blasi, Mike Larmer and Mike Brooks were joined with Tommy Bilyeu, James Blakey and Darrell Hover to form a strong team. The main asset was pitcher Steve Murdaugh, like me, a freshman at SMS. The best part of the '69 season was at the end when Young Men's team, First Baptist, picked Murdaugh and me to pitch for them in the Young Men's state tournament in Savannah. We had put together a couple of wins on Saturday before Steve joined us that evening after pitching a game or two in the Joplin Tournament that morning. With his awesome drop ball, Murdaugh was the most dominate pitcher in the tournament. He was also a very good hitter and after throwing all the games in Joplin and one in the tournament he applied a lavish amount of Icy Hot to his shoulder. He found out it was very uncomfortable to wear a shirt so he played left field in one game bare chested. After throwing a victory on Saturday night we lost the winner's bracket finals to the very good home team Savannah with "Murt" hurling a shutout for eight innings before losing 1-0 in nine. We had two runners thrown out between third base and home during the contest. We lost in the finals 3-0 to the excellent pitching of Kirby Hatcher, a pitcher to be reckoned with later on when playing for some great St. Joe Walnut Products teams. I spent a lot of time with Murdaugh that weekend and since he had driven up Highway 71 from Joplin by himself he asked me to ride home with him. The beginnings of that friendship proved to have a big impact not only on my softball career but also on my life in general.

# NINE

## OLD CROWE TRAVELIN' SHOW

Changes were in the works for the 1970 AAA league. Longtime sponsors Barnes Store and Empire Bank ceased their involvement and the league was faced with starting the season with only five teams. It was decided that the three top returning teams from last year's AA league would be brought into AAA. That decision sounded the death knell for the junior league but brought lots of new faces and talent to the top level. Har-Bell Sporting Goods, owned by former players Glenn Bell and Shorty Harrison, took over sponsorship for the Empire Bank team, but the Barnes players spread themselves out over the remaining teams with Jim Little's Scenic Shopper acquiring big hitters Bonus Frost and Jerry Bernet. Pitcher/manager Larry Atwood, Sammy Potter, Tom Majors and Steve Hutchinson all joined the Foremost team.

One of the teams moving up was the Hiland Dairy team, now to be sponsored by Crowe's Restaurant's. Business manager Ray Drennon thought the team could be better so it was decided the top three hitters from AA would be asked to come on board along with another pitcher. Bill Bishoff, Jerry Escabar and Mike Cluck were the three hitters and they readily agreed. I received an invitation that I always assumed came from the insistence of Steve

Murdaugh, so at the age of 19 I joined the league and reached one of my goals. The Crowe's team was young but had some hitting, pretty good defense and promising pitching. We were competitive on nights that Murt had his control, but runs against top throwers in the league were hard to come by and we finished 9-16 for the year. One of the highlights of the year was a tournament in Indianapolis, Indiana. Ray Drennon, who in retrospect was, in appearance and demeanor, a cross between Danny DeVito and Boris Badinoff of the Rocky and Bullwinkle cartoons, had gotten us into the highly rated tournament by lying about our record for the year. When asked what our record was Ray told them 42-12. The director said "that sounds pretty good" and Ray responded, "Sounds good to me too!"

Murt won the first game and we faced off against a really good Cincinnati team and ace pitcher Edmore Johnson. Ed was huge and moved at a slow pace but his pitches didn't. Edmore would later show up in Springfield in the late '70s pitching for Jim Little's team. He made quick work of our hitters, allowing one hit by pickup outfielder Dave Smoot. He also lashed a line drive between first base and second that nearly knocked 250-pound right fielder Jerry Escabar off his feet as he caught it. Both infielders said they never saw the ball it was driven so hard. We were watching one of Cincinnati's games when they were disputing a rule call. The manager tried to show the umpire the rule book but it was grabbed from his hand and thrown over the fence. It looked like every player jumped onto the fence trying to catch it on the fly. As on most road trips the team cleaned up for a night on the town. Being underage for any drinking I decided to stay at the motel and get some rest. We had also picked up Harve Welch from the Pepsi-Cola team and he was irritated that I wasn't joining the festivities so he hurled a Gideon's Bible at me as he left the room. One of my roommates on the trip was Drennon. He had already consumed several beverages and came out of the shower naked carrying a towel and walked around the room talking at great length. Mike Cluck sat in a chair beside the door and every time Ray turned his back Mike would completely open the door to the parking lot. When Ray turned back around he would close the door but kept right on talking. This scenario repeated itself several times. Cluck reported that he and Ray were sitting at a bar and one of the patrons was trying to engage in conversation with them. Finally, Ray turned to him and said, "That's not my line, you shitbird!" ending any further attempts at congeniality. We won the first game the next day before being ousted from the tournament. I threw a one hitter against defending champ Indianapolis and won on Robert Rice's fifth inning home run. I remember Mike Larmer in left field making some great catches to preserve the win. I gave up two hits the final game but we lost 3-1. I had thrown well in the tournament and had proven to myself that I could compete at a high level.

Pitchers warmed up in front of the bleachers along the first and third base lines. That provided a great observation point to see the pitches move and gauge how good the thrower was. I loved that portion of the pre-game, and it was always enjoyable to show off a little bit if you were pitching. I could always throw the ball well over handed and had learned enough from Hillcrest High School baseball coach Dick Birmingham to be able to fashion a pretty decent curveball. We were taught to hold the ball with the forefinger slightly off the seam with the middle finger providing the grip. The ball was brought directly over the top making the pitch drop rather than curve. Mark Gann took over catching duties in year two and our warm up ritual never changed. I would begin getting lose throwing the ball overhand and making it move in or out and then would toss in a few overhand drop balls. After that I began my underhand deliveries and with Gann's pinpoint accuracy I would give him a target to return the ball. Either holding my glove behind my back or between my legs, Gann's throws never missed and I didn't have to move my glove or body to make the catch. I don't know if any of the spectators ever noticed but we both took great delight in the display.

The second year for the Crowe's team revealed a much better defense and improved speed and hitting. We also brandished new uniform tops with a logo copied from an Old Crow Whiskey label fashioned by Ray Drennon. With Steve Hutton now playing shortstop full time, Mike Larmer at third, Jim March at second, Mike Brooks at first, the addition of catcher Gann gave us an airtight infield. Robert Rice, Dickie Curbow and Bob Hensley joined Pat Blasi and Jerry Escobar in the outfield to provide adequate defense and additional hitting. Kent McDaniel was an additional infielder and good hitter. Hensley turned in the defensive play of the year and maybe of all time. We were playing Foremost and Jim McDaniel sent a towering drive toward the left field fence. Bob took off for where the ball might come down but at the last second overran it. With his back to the infield he looked over his left shoulder but the ball was to the other side. He reached up with his right hand and bare handed the ball over his right shoulder and slammed into the fence. Everyone ran to the outfield to see if he was alright but as we arrived Bob leapt to his feet and sprinted back through his concerned teammates to his seat on the bench. An amazing catch!! We were improved with a year of experience, but two teams had dropped from the league cutting it to six clubs, which meant the remaining teams were all stronger adding good players and pitchers from the other teams. We had gotten better but still could not advance beyond the district tournament. What we turned out to be was a really good road team.

 The trip to Oklahoma City was a long drive from Springfield especially if you have six guys crammed into an 88 Oldsmobile. With Kent at the wheel, Rice, Curbow, brother Jim and I arrived at Doling Park to pick up Gann. It was fairly early in the year and we were not really that well acquainted with him. He had attended religious Evangel College so we did not know how he might react to our supply of beer for the trip. Our fears were eased when he appeared with a large cigar in his mouth and fell right in with us. We were hurdling down I-44 between Tulsa and Oklahoma City when Rice said he had to go to the bathroom. Not willing to stop and a little tipsy, his cousin Kent told him to piss out the window. After some readjusting in the back-seat he managed to get a partial leg outside the window and relieved himself. We had picked up great hitter Don Marrs from the Newspaper team and Donnie Hayworth from Foremost to cover for a couple of guys who couldn't make the trip. Our manager, "Doc" Blakey, was a professor at Evangel and didn't start either one of them the first game but by the third inning they were both in the lineup. It turned out to be a good thing and we one won all three games Saturday to qualify for the finals Sunday.

 As usual, most of us dressed to the nines to go out for the evening. Marrs and Haworth were several years older than the rest of us and decided to show us "the ropes" of the Ok City nightlife.

Oklahoma had much different liquor laws than Missouri, so we all pitched in to buy a club membership for Marrs and the rest of us could get in as guests. The club turned out to be a strip bar and when Mike Brooks realized it he thought we shouldn't go in. He was riding with Jim March who quickly stated, "This car's going in!" So Brooksy was pretty well stuck there for the evening. I followed Kent McDaniel who made his way rapidly to one of the front tables. He sat down with a group of gentlemen and told them how much better the dancers were on down the street. They fell for the idea and we quickly filled the tables nearest the stage. Murt, March and Curbow sat closest to the strippers and got most of the teasing right in their faces. Sitting on the other side of the table Kent turned to me and said, "I hope Murdaugh doesn't unleash Tremendous Tom on them!" A little later one of our players did the forbidden and groped one of the dancers causing a yell for security. All was settled quickly but the player said it was the fastest he had ever sobered up.

We played well in the final game but lost to the host Oklahoma City team 4-2. Jim "Spare" March launched a home run over the nearly 300-foot wall in left becoming only the second player to ever hit one out of the park. The first homer was hit a few years earlier by our pick-up player Don Marrs. We ran into the same Ok City team later that year in the Joplin Tournament and beat them. During the game Rice had singled to right field and hot dogged it down to first base. That didn't sit well with Ok City and on the next pitch their catcher (who had been given the derisive nickname by Springfield players of Charley "All World" Harris) gently tossed the ball to the first baseman. Rice was standing nonchalantly on the bag when the large first sacker Reggie Cleveland slammed the glove and ball into his stomach doubling him over. Rice didn't dog so much after that. Later in the game, with Mike Larmer at the plate, "All World" took a spit and part of it hit Larmer on the arm. Mike turned and spat squarely into the catcher's face. It took a several minutes to untangle that mess.

Topeka Plantation Steakhouse was the host team for the Topeka tournament. Their credentials included a couple of regional championships and national appearances and always strong showings in any games. Their pitching had included, from time to time, Charley Shlesinger. Billy Ray Jackson and Charley Rappard.

Their top thrower when we took them on was Rappart. He was 6'7", threw a big slingshot drop and, as Bob Hensley noted, looked like a large Griffin. They had some great hitters, Larry Elliot, Les Newman, Henry "Hawk" Murphy, Mike Simpson and Mike Flanagan, that all packed plenty of power. Mr. Harold Adams, the head umpire, actually played for them at one time. I refer to him as "Mr." not because of his size, 6'4" and 290 pounds, but because of his class and complete control of every ballgame he umped. Bob Hensley was called out at first base on a close call and came back to argue the call with Adams who was working the plate. In a booming voice he told Bob, "You couldn't be talking to me." Apparently Bob didn't quite get it and continued his plea. The second response was even louder and shook the benches, "You couldn't possibly be talking to me!!" Hensley crawled meekly back to his seat on the bench. Mr. Adams had been a really good hitter in his playing days and was behind the plate one day when he called a strike on Bob McLish. McLish turned and said, "You missed that one." Adams replied, "If I had the bat I wouldn't have!"

We played well in the tournament winning some close games. After a middle of the game rain delay against a good Jefferson City team, Mike Brooks game to the plate with a runner on second and stroked the first pitch from John Watkins up the middle to drive in the only run in the game. Murdaugh edged the host team in the winner's finals 2-1. The winning run scored when pickup player Richie Hubbard reached first base, stole second, and was bunted to third. Mike Larmer hit a pop fly to short left so shallow it was caught by shortstop Mike Simpson. Richie tagged up at third and scored on what was basically an infield fly. Mr. Adams told the next hitter, "That's the fastest white man I ever saw." I started the final game against Topeka and with Simpson at the plate decided to throw a rise ball by him up and in. Simpson lined it over the left field fence for a three-run lead. The next time up I felt it was important to teach him a lesson and throw the same pitch by him. The same result left us behind six to nothing. Jim March nailed a two-run homer later in the game to make it 6-2 and we rallied in the last inning to take an 8-6 lead. Murt relieved in the seventh inning but got into some trouble, so with the bases loaded and two out he was facing Rappard with a 3-2 count. He delivered another borderline drop on the outside and Mr. Adams called it a strike to end the game and we had won our first big tournament. No one, including Rappard, disputed the call out of respect for the umpire.

# TEN

## EVERYBODY LOVES RADER

The year of 1971 had seen Scenic Shopper play host to the national tournament and finish in the middle of the pack. The newspaper won the state championship and took second at the regional, losing to eventual national champion Cedar Rapids, Iowa. Scenic manager Jim Little wanted to make some changes to make his team a national contender. He procured the services of pitcher Gary Hutchens from Illinois and lured top hitters Don Marrs, Jim Maggi and Wayne Ryan from News and Leader. Hutch was a top-notch hurler with a quick hopping rise ball that moved late and eluded bats at the top portion of the strike zone. Hutch had wide shoulders and long arms and stood on top of shoes that stuck out to each side and looked like they came off of a circus clown. He was the first pitcher I had seen that swung his arm backward before stepping forward and throwing windmill. It was fortunate for Hutch that he could throw underhanded because he possessed zero other athletic abilities. He wisely refused to try to field ground balls and moved away from them as much as possible. But, he could really pitch and his team won the state and the regional with him on the mound. The additions to Scenic joined with Bonus Frost, Jerry Bernet, Jr. Williams, Jim Johnson, Jimmy

White and Larry Hale to form, in my opinion, the best starting lineup Springfield ever produced.

At the same time Sammy Potter decided to sponsor his own team and persuaded Steve Murdaugh and several other former Crowe's players to join him. Sammy also raided the Newspaper team and added Stan Shank, Denver Dixon and Tom Majors. Slugger Bob McLish, Jim McDaniel and Donnie Haworth added even more muscle to Potter's squad. Artie Charle and manager Larry Atwood provided pitching backup.

Ray Drennon had kept busy over the winter after he discovered the defection of, as he called them, "Murdaugh and his disciples", and found a new sponsor, ICH, and a new manager in Ronnie Shank. Ray hosted a meeting to organize the team built around pitchers Gene Barr, R.C. Crowe and Jim Collins. That was the complete staff from the Scenic national tournament team from the year before. Little had let steady right fielder Harold Harris go from his team and he and third baseman Jim Rader and catcher Jr. Williams were being courted to play. Gary Edwards from the Pepsi-Cola team was recruited to play short and Pat Blasi, Tom Lemons and Steve Cobb were asked to join the club along with the Hubbard brothers, infielder Richie and catcher Ronnie. Robert Rice jumped from Scenic to play shortly after the season started. I was added as the fourth pitcher because, for some reason, Ray liked me. I was not at the level of the other pitchers so it wasn't likely I would get much work but at the time it was my only option.

During the meeting Shank suggested that I lose some weight to help my throwing. I agreed to try and by season's start I had lost 20 pounds and found that Ronnie was right. I continued my diet and I trimmed down to 175 pounds, a total loss of 80 pounds a year and a half later.

Ray had ordered in the latest style of uniforms. Pinstriped, double knit pants and shirts, white with black stripes and gold lettering along with double knit caps. We played two exhibition games at Joplin in a light rain and as the games continued the hats kept shrinking until they looked like beanies by the last innings. After the game Rader went to Drennon and said, "Old double knit wasn't supposed to be caps, Ray. You better order something different." We had new hats the next week.

I wasn't the fourth pitcher very long. R.C. and Jr. rejoined Scenic opening night and Barr didn't fare well with our shaky infield defense and left at midseason to play for News and Leader. Catcher Ronnie Hubbard pretty much taught me how to compete at a higher level. He discovered I had a really good change up and started using it a lot to keep hitters off balance. I had developed the change/curve ball after watching "Black Jack" Kasanavoid use one effectively the year he threw in Springfield but had hardly used it. I threw a rise ball that moved and with the change showing the same spin my rise looked a lot quicker than it actually was. Now getting to pitch at least once a week and on most weekends and relying on Hubbard's knowledge of hitters, I quickly became an effective thrower. Rice and I soon found out what a great, somewhat cynical, sense of humor Rader had and we quickly relayed any overheard Raderisms to each other. I was warming up beside Jim at practice when 240-pound David Trotter came loping by wearing a pair of the old gray sweatpants. As he went by Rader quipped, "Gee, Dave, I've never seen a 300-pound sack of potatoes before!" He didn't get a reply.

At early practices Jim Collins had been throwing really hard for the time of year. I asked Rader how Collins could throw so well in the cool weather. Jim said, "He has probably been at his farm tossing some balls off the silo." Collins was a good thrower with speed and pitches that moved but sometimes lost confidence during the game after a hit or error. He had been a star basketball player in high school and was built like a wedge. At about 6'4" with wide shoulders and long arms, he was an imposing figure on the mound. Jim was mild mannered and endured a season or two of being the butt of Rader's observations. We were in the middle of a tight game with a runner on first and no one out when he turned to Rader at third, hid his mouth with the side of his glove and whispered the obvious, "Watch out for the bunt." Rader placed his glove at the side of his face and announced in a loud voice, "I love you too, Jim!!" We were playing Scenic one night and we were short of players. It was my turn to pitch, but Collins refused to play outfield so I got the assignment. We were shelled 19 to 2 in five innings. Left fielder Tom Lemons said he considered just crawling over the fence and going home. The team came in to bat in the fifth inning and Rader encouraged everyone to stay positive with his statement, "Come on, guys, four or five grand slams and we are right back in it!" Later in the year, Shank realized that catcher Hubbard had consumed too many beers to play. Shank had to catch and someone playing the next game asked Rader how things were going and he replied, "Pretty good. Shank keeps trying to throw the ball into center field and Collins keeps knocking it down."

After a very disappointing first half of the season, we settled in and became a pretty good softball team. A fan asked Rader what the sponsor ICH stood for and he explained, "Apparently, I Can't Hit." We qualified for the state tournament with Collins defeating the Newspaper team 5-3 in eight innings to place third in the district tournament. It would be my first trip to the state championship since joining the league. We finished state play winning two then being eliminated by Jefferson City and pitcher John Watkins 1-0 with Collins throwing a good game but losing. During one of our games Collins was standing outside the head high chain link fence beside brother Jim and Mike Larmer who was to play the next game. Collins sneezed and his chin came down on two of the barbs on top of the fence puncturing the skin and causing a lot of blood. Larmer had to walk away, overcome by laughter. Scenic won the state defeating Potter's and pitcher Steve Murdaugh in the finals and went on to win the regional and play in the nationals for their third consecutive year.

We traveled to Topeka again but with little success. Steve Hutsell had made the trip with us and volunteered to drive his big Dodge. We had gotten lost for a short time in Kansas City and in frustration Rice had taken the wheel. We ran into a rain storm between KC and Topeka and discovered the windshield wipers didn't work. We inched along the interstate until we were passed by a semi and Rice followed behind watching the truck's taillights. On the trip back in the 95-degree heat the car started heating up. We checked the oil and water and they were not the problem. It was decided the thermostat was out so we continued home at about 40 miles an hour with the heater on to diffuse the heat off the motor. It was a miserable trip but it worked and we limped home. At one point we were passed by a '62 Ford Falcon pulling a riding lawn mower — very embarrassing.

# Eleven

## Things Change

Over the winter the Hot Stove League was centered around Jim Little's bar, the Dugout Lounge, located on Main Street across the street from the demolished Santa Fe railroad depot. It was a good place to meet with friends and players from other teams and swap yarns, eat huge tenderloin sandwiches, and delve into the intricacies of red beer. A cold frosted mug was bottomed with an ounce of tomato juice then topped with draft beer. Slightly acidic, but otherwise smooth, it became my favorite beverage. On one evening's festivities Steve Murdaugh and I were discussing pitching and sports in general. He told me how he had been a pudgy kid and began exercising to be able to participate in high school athletics. I had established a good friendship with SMS basketball player Mike Keltner who was majoring in Phys Ed and we talked him into developing a workout program for us over the winter. With Murt's encouragement and involvement, we ran, lifted weights and threw to each other indoors for six months. One of our throwing areas was under the stands at the football stadium. It was dimly lit, usually had puddles of standing water, which made it humid and dank, and was not a fun place to catch Murt's heavy drop balls.

I was surprised one evening to find Steve had brought girlfriend Sue Schuble to catch us. Sue was one of SMS's first female athletes and played basketball, softball, volleyball, and anything else the administration would allow for women's sports. She caught hard thrower Cindy Henderson for the school team and they would win a national title before the NCAA took over the sport. The core of that team played together under the Foremost sponsorship and played in several state and regional tournaments. I was impressed that not only could she catch me easily but handled Murt's nasty pitches very well.

ICH had changed its name to Ozark National Life so we got a new name but retained pretty much the same team. Stan Shank and Billy Bain joined the team and we became better defensively and at the plate. Outfielder Tom Lemons became a target of Rader's good-natured jokes. Once when Tom popped a medium fly ball to right and Jim jumped to his feet yelling, "Get outta here! Get outta here!" Tom perked up rounding first then realized it was just an easy out. In another game, Lemons rolled a weak grounder between short and third during a contest we were losing badly. Jim noted loudly to the bench, "Come on guys, don't make Tommy do it all." One night I was throwing and Tom had been complaining of a head cold accompanied with a runny nose. Tom caught a routine fly ball in left field and when the ball came back in Jim yelled, "Nice play, Tommy," then turned to me and said, "You know Tommy has a cold." I just shook my head and stated, "Wow, what a man." It was the only time I can remember ever making Rader laugh.

We started the year very strong, finishing second in the first half. Scenic had acquired pitcher Steve Neilson from Kansas City to replace Gary Hutchins but he was not of the same caliber. In our second meeting our guys drilled him for nine runs going into the last inning. I had held them to two runs until they rallied in the last of the seventh for three more runs with one out and runners on base. Manager Ronnie Shank came to the mound, I assumed, to take me out. But instead left me in saying, "I want you to finish this game so you know and they know you can beat them." It was a badly needed boost to my ego. I managed to get the final two outs and notched the victory. Ronnie's words turned out to be very prophetic as I became a thorn in their side for the next several years. My teams didn't always beat them but we were always competitive against what turned out to be one of the top three or four clubs in the nation.

The second half of the year was a grind, with us playing through a team-wide batting slump and getting subpar defensive and pitching efforts. The Foremost team caught fire and ripped through the second half, tying Scenic for the league lead. With Gene Barr on the mound and great hitting they became a formidable opponent. They went into the last inning of a playoff game leading by two runs with runners on second and third and Bob McLish coming to the plate. After a consultation on the mound they decided to pitch to Bob instead of walking him and putting the winning run on base. McLish sent an offering from pitcher Shelby Hill over the right field fence to get the walk off win.

Our Ozark National team peaked for the district defeating a good News Leader team and Foremost for an undefeated run to the tournament title. Our luck changed at the state tournament going a disappointing 2-2 and watching Jefferson City Rippeto win the title over St. Joseph Walnut Products behind the pitching of John Watkins.

1969 News and Leader

Front row: C.B. Freeman, Richie Hubbard, Mike Dickey, Ted West, Phil Groover, Leon Bischoff, Tim Buff

Back Row: Buddy Foell, Bob Mclish, Stan Shank, Carl Cox, Kenny Williams, Ron Crosswhite, Denver Dixon

Late in the summer the Foremost team was playing a tournament in Yates Center, Kansas, and was needing another pitcher for Sunday. Manager Ancil Fry called and asked me to come out and said that Gene Barr would be by to give me a ride. Even though Barr and I had been teammates for part of a season I really didn't know him very well and was happy to get the chance to spend a little time with my idol. Gene and girlfriend Barb Harris picked me up and sped at 90 miles an hour to eastern Kansas with Barb at the wheel. We arrived in time and I won my game over Joplin Industrial Electric before Barr made short work of Topeka Plantation Restaurant for first-place. Wayne Ryan had driven out with Steve Hutton and Charlie Essary but needed me to drive them home after Wayne had procured a case of beer after the game. I had never driven a car with a manual transmission so, after finally getting it going, I made it pretty well until we hit a stoplight in Carthage, Missouri. After several unsuccessful attempts to move forward Charlie had to take the wheel and get us home.

A week or two later our Ozark National team was playing in the Columbia, Missouri, tournament. We were short a couple of players and Shank asked Ancil to fill in at third base. We were facing league rival Lebanon in a loser's bracket game when Barr arrived to throw against us as a pickup player. I was the recipient of a 4-3 loss, with Gene getting the victory and driving in the winning run late in the contest. After the game I found Ancil or "Spike" as everyone called him at the motel bar and invited him to join us in our room with our ample supply of "cold ones". I was enthralled with Spike's rich archive of softball memories and narratives, which could only be obtained by applying a mix of cigarettes and beer. I had watched Ancil play for years and was amazed on more than one occasion to see him slide into a base and have cigarettes and matches fly from beneath his cap as it came off his head. Much later Spike told me he had played third base for 40 years, and 22 of those years were with the same Foremost Dairy sponsor. That night he held us riveted to his every word from batting against Clarence "Buck" Miller and Aurora, Illinois, ace Harvey Sterkel to playing in the outlawed International Softball Conference tournaments under assumed names like Roy Tan and the Boyd brothers. He also told of his early exploits with best friend pitcher Tim Buff, whom he always called "Dude". They were such close friends they each named their sons after each other. Spike went from being Mr. Fry, coach, to teacher to high school principal to school superintendent in the daytime, but still third baseman at any other time. I have never met anyone who loved the sport more than Spike or who enjoyed talking about it as much.

Late in the evening Ronnie Shank got a phone call informing him that Barr and Barb had lost their lives in car wreck near Eldon, Missouri. Gene had to return to Springfield to throw his morning paper route and was asleep in the back seat when the accident occurred. We were all shocked by the news and the party was quickly over with each of us left to silently absorb our loss. My idol's life had ended at age 36. In the world of softball his accomplishments were great. He pitched the entire 24-inning loss for Barnes Store in the 1959 nationals, still the second longest game in ASA history, losing 2-0 on an error. The next year, pitching for A and A Shopette, he helped the team to a fifth-place finish, throwing 38 innings in four games. His losses were to eventual champion Clearwater, Florida, in 15 innings, losing on an error 1-0. He came back the next day to no-hit powerhouse Aurora, Illinois, again losing 1-0 on an unearned run. During his astounding tournament he allowed nine hits, no earned runs, and only six outs were recorded by the outfield. Nasty drop ball indeed!

# TWELVE

## BALLPARKS

My first road trip was to Savannah, Missouri, for the Young Men's State Tournament. There was really nothing of note from that trip except a second-place finish and the only home run I ever hit. I caught a waist high drop ball and sent it over the left field fence at a park in nearby Amazonia. Bartlesville, Oklahoma, was the next trip with Crowe's Restaurants. There were two fields, both facing the same direction, with the left field fence of one park abutting the first base stands of the other field. The first visit was short. We didn't play very well, but outfielder Pat Blasi homered in one game, hitting a spectator in park two in the back. Catcher Mike Cluck came back to the bench to report a conversation he had heard from a team waiting to play the next game. I had been pitching with Robert Rice warming up along the outfield foul line. One player asked the other how the pitching looked and he responded, "The guy throwing is slow and the one warming up is even slower." Cluck took an excessive amount of glee in relaying that information to us.

One memorable aspect of the complex was the sale of Coors beer at the concession stand. Coors was outlawed in Missouri at the time under the guise that it was not pasteurized. More likely, the considerable lobbying of the Anheiser-Busch company had kept the competition out of state. At the time it was a big deal to have it so available to us and we took advantage of the opportunity. A couple of years later Jim Collins and I were picked up by Sav-Mor Markets to pitch in the tournament. We had finished a game and Steve Hutton, Kent McDaniel and I were sipping some Coors and watching one of the other Springfield teams, 89er Restaurant, play. There was a close play at third and the Springfield player popped up from his slide and he and the third baseman became involved in a pushing contest. Two of the Springfield wives came out of the stands and on to the field to protect their men. One of the irate wives was a mousey gal who seldom spoke to anyone in the crowd much less an opposing team. I guess she was caught up in the excitement as she screamed out a stream of obscenities we had never before heard connected." She had to be led off the field by her husband who draped his arms over her trembling shoulders reminding me of an image of a caped, emotionally drained, James Brown being helped off the stage. We stared at each other in disbelief at the spectacle before practically falling off the bleachers in laughter.

With a runner on first the batter singled to left with Stu Dunlop picking up the ball and hurling it toward third. Stu had a strong, but somewhat erratic, throwing arm and with the third base coach waving the runner to third Stu's throw hit the coach in the forearm with the ball. Third sacker Rod Towe chased the ball down in time to throw out the runner trying to score. We saw the coach the next day with a cast on his arm. Dunlop had broken a bone with his toss. There was no love lost between St. Joe and Springfield teams and fans. After Empire Bank had lost a loser's bracket game at Drake the announcer boomed over the microphone "And the last Springfield team bites the dust!" At that point Crosswhite picked up a small rock and tossed it at the press box hitting the announcer squarely between the eyes. The team made a hasty retreat before the police could arrive.

The Walnut Product field was privately owned and was the nicest park in the state. The company sponsored several teams and they were always prominent in state and regional tournaments. The only negative to the park was that it was built in an industrial area and the odor of sulphur hung in the air along with a good supply of flies on hand. The park served up a lot of Pearl beer and the fans were usually obnoxious if you were the visiting team. We were sitting in the bleachers watching the state tourney with the newspaper's catcher Teddy West close by. As the rest of the News and Leader team assembled there before warming up Jim Maggi and his pretty wife Alice sat down near us. Ted, with a jaw full of tobacco, joked, "There wasn't a fly up here 'til Alice Maggi sat down!" Maggi enjoyed the remark much more than the prim Alice did.

We had played the really good Walnut Product team to a 0-0 tie going into the last inning and, with two strikes on shortstop Charlie Pusitari, Mark Gann signaled for a rise ball up and away. I instead decided to jam him inside when Pus reminded me of why Gann was such a good catcher as he lined the ball over the left field fence resulting in a one run loss. We were short of players that game and Walnut's former left fielder was in attendance. Horton talked him into playing the game for us but sometime during the game the police arrived at our dugout looking for him. The players on the bench pointed to left field but it was vacant of an outfielder. Some of them said they saw him scrambling over the wooden fence when he saw the police showed up. I don't know if Horton ever got the uniform back.

Jefferson City used three fields for competition in tournament play. Eagle's field was not a lucky place for any of the teams I played for, but I never pitched a game there. Vivian was the baseball park and I hated it. To turn in a lineup you had to climb a steep angled ladder and then ascend a steep roof to the press box. I never attempted the climb. The mound was always raised and the plate was set, it seemed to me, slightly off center from the pitching rubber. It was a great field for drop ball throwers but not for me. I never felt comfortable on the mound and I can't remember ever getting a win there, although several guys I played with enjoyed a lot of success. The remaining field was down the hill from the baseball park resting in a hollow with a small creek running outside the left field fence. Duensing park was always humid and stale with little air movement, but I always pitched well there. I can only remember one loss and that was in a relief stint. We defeated then defending state champion Jeff City Rippeto there early one year as I threw a one hitter. Their only run was on my error as I fielded a bunt with a runner on second and threw it past first baseman Mike Brooks allowing the runner to score.

Jeff City was hosting a tournament one year when a Shriners' convention resulted in a lack of rooms for the teams. Mike Brooks, brother Jim and I were given sleeping quarters at tournament director Jim Veith's ex-wife's home. Brooksy slept in a girl's room with lots of pink decoration. Jim and I got the boy's room complete with a caged hamster that kept us awake most of the night running in its wheel. St. Louis Kutis was in town and at a game at Duensing field manager Norb Thurmer went into a tirade coaching third base. Norb always reminded me of cartoon character Foghorn Leghorn with his booming voice and physical presence. He had a habit of turning his head to the side while rotating his shoulder and extending his arm when on a roll and these gestures became more and more pronounced the madder he got. The last ball had been fouled out of play and each team was asked to produce two balls each to continue play. His response was, "We come down here to play ball and you don't have any damn rooms or damn balls! What kind of tournament you got here?" Norb was scary at first sight but was really a great guy when you got to know him. One of his favorite sayings to his hitter was, "You're better than he are." Shortstop Steve Hutton retorted, "Hell, Norb, he ain't even better than I are."

# Thirteen

## The Five Hitter

The 1973 season ended with Scenic-Gaslight defending their Regional Tournament championship and finishing fourth in the nationals in Seattle, Washington. The team picked up pitchers Kenny Williams and "Doc" Miller from Savannah and added Phil Wilkerson to the squad. Kenny Williams was awesome in the tournament and Bob McLish provided the lumber needed by blasting five homeruns and driving in thirteen on his way to being selected Most Valuable Player and setting records in both categories. Not satisfied with the result, manager Jim Little acquired the services of hard throwing Jack Burkhart from Kansas City and arguably the best pitcher in the world, Roy Burlison.

Our Ozark National team had walked through the district tournament with our closest game against a very good open league team, Hamlin Insurance, sponsored by former AAA player and manager Jack Hamlin. We had won when Richie Hubbard stole second on a highly debated call and came around to score the winning run. The young Hamlin team featured speed and hitting with a solid defense. Steve Stewart and Gary Augustine did the mound work with Steve "Stump" Stombaugh behind the plate. The infield consisted of Gary Stracke, Gary Palmer, Rick Jackson and

Alan Potts. The very fleet outfield was made up of Steve Baker, Buddy Young, Jim Logan and Mike Wolf. Ironically, the Hamlin team was ousted from the city tournament when they were defeated by another open league team the Queen City Flyers, a team I had managed throughout the summer. The Flyers were anchored by Rod Towe, Randy Johnson, Virgle Fredrick, Mike Teague, Byron McDaniel, Mike Brooks, Mike Larmer, Ted Linke, Mike Keltner, and pitcher Jim Horton. A good team in its own right.

The Ozark National team split apart with players going to the other four AAA teams while manager Ron Shank agreed to coach the Hamlin team's upward advance to the league. The league would consist of only five teams, with Hamlin joining Gaslight, News and Leader, Frost's Sporting Goods, and Foremost. I was recruited by Shank to pitch and we also added speedy Mike Keltner to replace the departing Buddy Young. On the bright side Springfield would be hosting the Regional Tournament with the league champion becoming the host team. With defending champ Gaslight already in the fold, Springfield would have at least two teams in the tournament and could add a third with a state winner. In addition, three district teams would qualify for state play.

The Hamlin players were very talented, laid back, somewhat irreverent, and overly sure of themselves. I tried to explain to them that the pitching and defense was much better night after night than they were accustomed to but to no avail. Besides Burkhart and Burlison, Gaslight had steady Gary McDaniel on the mound while News and Leader could throw Steve Murdaugh, Tim Buff and Jack Dennis at you. Frost's featured Jim Collins and Russ Strunk, while Foremost had Gary Augustine and Shelby Hill pitching for them. Every league game would be a struggle against top pitchers, powerful hitters and good defenses. The Frost's team was an accumulation of former Lebanon, Ozark National, and News and Leader players. One of those added to the Frost's team was power hitting catcher Louie Bunch. Aside from being a feared hitter Louie possessed the best throwing arm I had ever seen. Bob Turner and Donnie Haworth had great arms from the shortstop position, and Jim Smith, Don Marrs and Oliver Smith were terrific from the outfield, but none of them could match the cannon Louie had from behind the plate.

Of my new teammates I bonded quickly with Jim Logan and fellow pitcher Steve Stewart. They both were very talented, intensely competitive, and willing to work to become better players. A few of us had gathered after a practice to grab a bite to eat when Logan told us about a kid's television show he had seen. The show was a hosted by a guy dressed up like a clown who called himself Clownie. There was a row of 4-year-olds seated on the set and Clownie would go down the line and converse with each one. After the chat he would ask if they wanted to kiss Clownie on his red nose. All of them obliged until he came to one of the last kiddies. He pointed to his rear end and said "kiss on this a while Clownie!" For ever after, Jim Logan has been called "Clownie" by his fellow players.

Just before the season was to begin Ron Shank informed the team he would not be managing. I was thrust into the position of pitcher/manager for the year. It was decided that Steve Stewart would coach during games that I was pitching, which led to an uneasy dance of mutual consideration and reluctant ascension. Whichever one of us was pitching, the other thrower had to decide when a pitching change was necessary and had to replace the pitcher. Most of the mound visits ended with, "You are doing great. Hang in there." Needless to say, not many pitching changes were made that year.

I did learn, after a lot of unenthusiastic practices, that the Hamlin guys were "gamers". They brought their best efforts at game time. I tried for several weeks to move 6'6", 280-pound first baseman Alan "Hap" Potts to the outfield and play Mike Keltner at the bag but it didn't work at either end. Potts wasn't comfortable in right field and Keltner showed a resistance to stick his nose in and take away the bunt from lefthanded hitters. Mike was adequate in the outfield but I had really underestimated the hands and agility of "Hap". With long arms and soft hands it was almost impossible to get a ball by him at first. He was one of the best defensive infielders I have ever played with — a happy surprise.

One of the first games of the year had us squaring off against Gaslight with their great offense and national reputation. As always when throwing against them I had to attempt to corral the adrenalin rushing through my veins. I had to throw at three quarters speed for a few innings until I settled down, and the ball moved everywhere. That night it moved into Larry Hale's side, Bonus Frost's arm — twice, just missed Bob McLish's head, found Denver Dixon's leg, and glanced off Beau Robinson's shoulder hitting him between the eyes. After all that, we entered the seventh inning leading 3-2. With two runners on and two outs I jammed Bonus, and he lifted a weak liner to short. The shortstop dropped the ball and, with runners going on contact, we couldn't get a force out. Bob McLish came up next and he lined a rise ball down the opposite field line to score the winning runs.

We finished the year 6-14 but were competitive in most games and the team improved steadily over the year. The newspaper team finished second in the league and hosted the regionals. We qualified for the state tournament in Jefferson City and in an unprecedented move picked up Danny O'Neal to manage us in the championship. We also picked up great hitter Rod Towe and pitcher Jerry Mallonee out of the open leagues to make the trip. Our first game was against a very good Joplin Revival Fires team built around the the Doss cousins, Leonard on the mound and good hitter Henry behind the plate. Fred Doss, Rick Sadler and Danny Wooliver added power and average at the plate. In an unusual decision in the first inning, with a runner on second and two outs, Joplin chose to intentionally walk Steve Stombaugh putting runners at first and second. Rod Towe was next up and lined a home run over the left center field fence. Stombaugh rounded the bases chanting, "Leonard Skinnerd"eats a big one!" We held on to win 3-2, with Jerry Mallonee relieving to get the last three outs. We finished the tournament with a 3-2 record, losing both games by one run. Jefferson City Rippeto repeated as state champions behind pitcher John Watkins. Gaslight defended their regional title defeating News and Leader in the all-Springfield title match. Roy Burlison finished the league season with an 8-0 record. The Hamlin team did not face him, but we saw pitcher Jack Burkhart quite enough. There would be big changes in the league the following year.

## FOURTEEN

## MOUSEY'S

Jefferson City won a state championship in the '50s. It took 20 years for them to repeat and they did those two years in a row, winning back-to-back titles in 1973 and 1974. The only tie between the teams was pitcher and manager "Mousey" Mathis. Mousey had been one of the best throwers in the state until an automobile accident caused several injuries. He never regained his prowess as a pitcher but was known statewide as a "character" on the field and in the stands. He occasionally clowned from the mound while sneaking up on good ball teams who enjoyed the show but ended up on the losing side. In the early '70s he built a formidable team featuring ace pitcher and top flight hitter John Watkins from southeast Missouri. Mousey added Lindon Duncan and Bill Parker from the same area along with local players Woody Taggart, Ron Beismeyer, Kelly Burre, Monty Clithero, Kelly Whittaker, and a good catcher built like a bowling ball named Jack Cannon. Jack was a good hitter and owed his strong physique to years of concrete work. His claim to fame in normal life was the work he had done in the construction of the Gateway Arch in St. Louis. The 1974 team also had added pitcher Steve Neilson after his one-year stay in Springfield. The club had a lot of power at the plate, a solid defense with Clithero covering two thirds of the outfield from his center field position and a party atmosphere, except during games that mattered. Several times during those years we often stayed at the same motels during tournaments and I was always amazed that a team that stayed up and drank so hard at night could get back on the field the next day and perform at such a high level.

In our Crowe's Restaurant days Ray Drennon had called to enter the team in the Jeff City tournament. Ray said that communicating with Mousey was like talking to a Redd Foxx record! I am not certain, but I believe his nickname came from his facial features with small, squinty eyes and a fairly long thin snout. Mousey circulated the Kansas City Star newspaper for the Jefferson City area and accumulated endless stacks of newspapers throughout his bachelor residence. Monte Clithero said that Mousey would sit in his favorite chair in the evening sipping his whiskey and occasionally picked up the 22 pistol he kept by his side to shoot at mice as they ran through the piles of newspapers. He had shut out a really good Foremost team in 1968 in the opening game of the state championship, and when the Foremost club arrived at the motel in Jefferson City the next year for Mousey's tournament he met them in the parking lot. He had thrown down a few drinks and really got on them about last year's game and how he was going to repeat that performance when they played the next morning. Jack Hasten turned to Ancil Fry and said, "I'm hitting the first pitch I see from that son of a bitch out of the park." Hasten was true to his word, and Mousey only lasted a couple of innings in the contest. I was witness to the last game he pitched in Springfield. After getting beat around pretty well he had taken himself out of the game and came around to the bleachers behind third base. Several of our team were sitting there waiting to play the next game when Mousey looked over at us and stated, "You know, everybody says your legs go first, but my mind went a long time ago" as he picked up his spikes and tossed them into a yard behind the fence, symbolically ending his pitching career.

Although Jeff City had won the state, the best team in the state and the region and a national tournament contender was Springfield's Gaslight Realty. With the addition of top flight pitchers Jack Burkhardt and Roy Burlison Gaslight had walked through the regional tournament and made a strong run for the national championship taking third-place. Burlison threw 45 great innings losing to Santa Rosa, California, and hurler K.C. Fincher 2-0 in 9 innings and to the perennial powerhouse Aurora, Illinois, Sealmasters and big lefthander Pete Carlson. Jack Burkhardt got a key victory in the tournament defeating pitcher Ty Stofflet and Reading, Pennsylvania. At the time, Stofflet was generally regarded as the best lefthanded pitcher, if not the best pitcher, in the country. He was slim and not physically imposing but possessed catlike quickness on the mound. He was built like a pair of wire pliers with strong legs, extra-long arms and huge hands. He had also developed a devastating change to go along with a quick rise ball and a nasty drop that went away from right-handed hitters. Stofflet worked as an electrician for Mack Trucks. He only donned the mask and cape for big time softball tournaments.

    I had taken a job with a local produce market and, although I hadn't had the time to work out as I had the past couple of years, the loading and unloading of trucks had made me stronger than before. That was my favorite part of the job. One warm winter day Mike Keltner had come by the house and wanted to go over to the newly built outdoor basketball courts at Southwest Missouri State and shoot a few baskets, so Jim, Steve Hutsell and I accompanied him. Keltner really didn't need the practice. He played for the SMSU Bears and they had finished runner-up in the 1974 NCAA Division 2 finals. While we were there Jim Horton and Rod Towe came by to talk to me. Horton had gotten a sponsor to back a AAA team for the next summer and he needed a pitcher to build the team around. He already had one of the best players in town in Towe and also two of his open league teammates, Tom Smith and Fred Harrison. It was my best option at the time so I agreed. Horton asked for names of other players he could get and I gave him a list of guys I thought highly of and who might be available. Much to my surprise and delight, he convinced all of them to join the squad. Little did we know we would contend for the league and state titles the next season. Soon to take the field would be Horton's All-Stars.

## FIFTEEN

## HORTON'S

All the pieces had fallen into place. One player after another had agreed to join the Horton's until we had amassed what I thought was the best defensive team in the league. We would follow the route to success mapped out by predecessors Barnes Store, Empire Bank and Scenic Shoppers. Tight defense, speed, and aggressiveness on the bases could make up for any presumed lack of offense. Pitching was still a question mark, but the Park Board had done our team a great favor without realizing it. With an increase of slow pitch teams in the city it was decided that the fences at Fassnight would be moved from 250 feet to 275 feet. The softball gods had smiled down on us from their lofty heights.

1971 Scenic Shopper

Front row: Don McDaniel, Jim Little, Junior Williams, Ron Hubbard, Jim Rader, Jim Johnson, Jim White, Ron Shank, Lon McDaniel

Back Row: Ila Calfee, Larry Hale, Harold Harris, Joe Williams, Gene Barr, Ken Williams, R.C. Crowe, Joe Marler, Jim Collins, Hershel Hubbard, Roy Calfee

Steve Stewart, my fellow pitcher from the Hamlin team, was the choice to be the other hurler. Although his won/loss record from the year before did not reflect it, he improved over the season and had learned when to challenge hitters and when to pitch around them. He had a good head controlling his ego, which was very difficult to do for any pitcher, and possessed nerves of steel and confidence in his abilities. He was attending law school at the University of Missouri and wouldn't be immediately available, but we had Jim Horton to pick up some of the slack. Stewart, like all softball pitchers, had an extra-large throwing arm. Jim Logan often teased him about his "gorilla arm" but it was a badge of honor for pitchers. Gene Barr's left arm was above average in girth but his right could have been mistaken for one of Popeye's huge forearms. Drop ballers tended to have large forearms and generally took a shorter stride in an effort to get on top of the ball and tended to really drag their back foot on the release. Rise ball pitchers had to break their wrist to the side and usually had a large muscle bump on the outside of the throwing arm. A longer step helped them stay under the ball and the back foot came up rather than digging into the mound.

The best thing to aid the pitching staff was the addition of catcher Mark Gann. Gann had been nicknamed "Scrapper" by Steve Murdaugh back in the Crowe's Restaurant days for his ability to consistently dig Murt's heavy drop balls out of the dirt. He had caught Gene Barr for a year with Foremost with equal success controlling Barr's quick diving pitches. Built like a kangaroo with huge thighs Gann could catch effortlessly for inning after inning. He was deliriously happy when catching and decidedly pissed off when it was his turn to sit out a game. Scrapper moved the ball on offense and was fast from base to base. His biggest asset was the handling of pitchers and his uncanny ability to call games from his position. Wise throwers learned early to throw whichever pitch Gann called for and in the location he wanted. Your chances of success were greatly increased. He had taken a job teaching and coaching in Sullivan, Missouri, and would be 135 miles away until classes were out for the summer. The answer was Scrapper's Datsun Z28 sports car that could make the trip down I44 in less than two hours. We referred to the car as the Songbird, named after the plane on the old Sky King television show, and Mark was never late for a game.

First base would be handled by the astute and thrifty Mike Brooks. Mike made his living as a middle school science teacher. "Brooksy" practiced frugality in all things and he carried that over to the ballpark. He was focused at all times and never wasted movement or energy, was fundamentally sound with good hands and always with a plan. Playing against Jefferson City in the Topeka tournament, we were tied 0-0 with a runner on second base and two outs with "Brooksy" up facing John Watkins. The rain poured down and we were forced into a long delay. We retired to the motel but Mike never let go of his bat during the wait. The bat was pretty much illegal, looking like a car had driven over the barrel flattening it out. After the game resumed some two hours later "Brooksy" laced the first pitch back through the box driving in the only run of the game. Murdaugh told of a time in a restaurant when Mike was ordering orange juice and quizzed the server on prices and sizes of the small and medium drinks. Not satisfied with her response he asked her to bring out the two glasses so he could determine the best buy. Actually, it was just all part of his understated sense of humor.

Jim March would handle the second base position. He was the sixth man on his high school basketball team and was called "Spare", a nickname that carried over to the ballpark. He was employed at the newspaper and would work up to a district manager position in the circulation department before moving to a sales position with an electronics company. "Spare" possessed a good bat with lots of power. He was surprisingly fast and had really quick hands. He referred to his glove as "The Old Pancake" because it was broken in completely flat using it to trap the ball with his throwing hand giving him a quick release. Shoulder surgery to eliminate an aneurism had left him unable to throw over the top so he developed a side arm slinging motion that was extremely effective. Jim had a very derisive sense of humor, and Steve Hutton called him the "Old Spiteful Spare".

One of the most, if not the most, dependable shortstops in the league was the sure handed Steve Hutton. Never flashy, Steve made every routine play and didn't make mental mistakes. He had some pop in his bat and was a good base runner. Coached by legendary baseball coach Dick Birmingham, Steve was fundamentally sound with great footwork at short and a quick release. Known from time to time as "Hoolie, Hutter, and Hooter", it was usually just "Hut" for short. Equipped with a quick wit and sharp tongue, few could weather his pin-pointed verbal assaults. "Hut" also worked at the newspaper in the advertising department. We were playing one night when short and fleet opposing center fielder Larry Earlywine was chasing down a line drive that had gotten between the outfielders and rolled to the right center fence. Steve noted that "Earlywine looked like a bunny rabbit headed for the briar patch!"

At third would be Gary Stracke. "Strac" had played with the Hamlin Insurance team in both open league and the previous year's AAA team. Solidly built, Gary was powerful at the plate and a quality defensive player. He also was one of only two players who were married at the time, the other being pitcher/manager Jim Horton. Stracke became a high school coach and teacher. He was comfortable batting in the middle of the lineup and had collected a lot of key hits and runs batted in. Like the rest of the squad, he was fundamentally sound at the plate, on the field, and on the base paths. Gary was laid back and easy going but was another player who really hated sitting out.

Horton had accumulated four excellent outfielders, Jim Logan, Tom Smith, Gus Henry and Rod Towe. Tommy had inherited his softball genes from his dad and uncles, the legendary Smith Brothers, who had starred in Springfield in the '50s with his father, Gene, playing into the late '60s. Defensively Tom was not fast but got great jumps on fly balls. He was sure handed with an accurate arm and patrolled right and center fields equally well. "T" was a certified .300 hitter year after year spraying line drives all over the park. He had a natural inside out swing that fit perfectly with his role as the number two hitter in the lineup, allowing him to hit behind base runners on steals and hit and run plays. Another big asset was his ability to play every position on the field, which helped rotate players in and out as needed. Tom was a radiology technician and also garnered the nickname "Quarren T" when his boast of having at least 20 beautiful nursing students at one of our team parties fell well short in all categories.

1950 City Champions St Joseph Church's Smith Brothers
Front row: Gene Smith, Walt Smith
Back row: Larry Smith, Joe Smith

Jim "Clownie" Logan, who could adapt to any of the outfield positions, was very reliable defensively. He had improved fundamentally over the year and learned quickly from the other players on the team. A good, accurate arm kept runners from advancing an extra base and saved more than a few runs. "Clownie" was strong and fast and naturally aggressive on the base paths and had great bat control, being able to bunt and slap the ball to the opposite field. Jim was the most loyal and competitive teammate I ever had. He never gave up or gave in. Quick to laugh and fast to ire, "Clownie" was all in for every game we played or at the first sign of possible fisticuffs at some of the bars we patronized back in the day. Playing in the finals of the state tournament one year Logan came to the plate with the tying run on third base and two outs. He hit a two hopper to the shortstop, which appeared to be a routine play and a loss, but "Clownie" flew down the line and beat the throw to tie the game. Jim was a gamer.

Then there was Gus Henry in centerfield. Gus had been recruited by Rod Towe who knew him from when they played baseball at Southwest Missouri State University. When baseball season had rolled around for Gus's second year, he had not appeared for any of the team meetings. Coach Bill Rowe had written a note on a blackboard at the entrance of the locker room that read, "Gus Henry — see coach Rowe." In a message scrawled beneath it was another statement, "Coach Rowe — see Gus Henry." Gus was the oldest son of former News and Leader catcher Denny Henry. His athletic ability was at a high level, with speed, power, great hands, strong arm and natural aggressiveness. At early practices Horton was trying to decide whether Gus or Rod should be the centerfielder. Gus said that it should be him and Rod questioned "Why is that?" Gus just laughed and said, "Because I'm a lot better than you", so Gus played center. He also played first base and was one of the best I had ever seen at that position. Very quick and with that great arm, he was almost impossible to bunt on. Gus was a metal worker and lived his life on the edge. He never attended a party he didn't like.

The left fielder for most games was Rod Towe. Rod was the best player I ever played with. He quickly became one of the most feared hitters in the league. Rod consistently batted over 300 for nearly 15 years and was excellent in the field. Besides being fundamentally sound and having a high understanding of the game, Rod, like Tom Smith, was versatile and could play every position, usually at a higher level than the player he was subbing for. Softball was seemingly made for Rod. Strong and short, he offered a small strike zone and was very aggressive at the plate. With that great hand-eye coordination he could hit whatever he swung at, sometimes pitches outside of the strike zone. Even though I preached to him about pitch selection time after time he never changed. If he had listened to me he would probably have hit .400 for those 15 years. Rod was hard-nosed but fair and didn't take shots at unprotected players. Overall, in my opinion, he was one of the best to ever play in Springfield.

Fred Harrison Jr. was a holdover from Horton's open league team. Actually, a pretty good ball player, Fred was on a team that would not afford him much playing time. He was valuable for being able to play multiple positions which worked out great for weekend play when we might be missing a player or two. We were socializing at our favorite watering hole one evening when the bar presented a large wheel of cheese for everyone's enjoyment. Fred came back to the table with only a couple of small pieces of cheese, and Rod asked him why he hadn't gotten more. Robert Rice quickly piped up and stated, "That was all he could gnaw off!" After that Rod pinned the nickname of "Cheezer" on him. Fred's dad, Fred Harrison Sr., was our unofficial scorekeeper. He never seemed to sit on the bench but preferred to squat down at the end of the seat. He was given the name of "Squats" by Jim March.

Jim Horton had obtained the necessary funds for a sponsorship, and Danny O'Neal had been lined up to manage the team. Danny bailed out early on so Jim became the business manager, third base coach and manager. Horton was a good business manager, a great third base coach, but had a few problems as manager when coping with a team of older, more experienced players. But he worked it out through the year. Jim could move the ball at the plate, was a decent thrower, and was fairly fast as a base runner. Spring would come early in 1975, so we started practice in February and were more than ready when league play began.

## Sixteen

### The Game

The '75 league looked like an easy lock for Jim Little's squad coming off their third-place finish at the national tournament and finding a new sponsor in Emerald Finance. Roy Burlison was back on board although Jack Burkhart had taken flight back to Kansas City. The newspaper was beefed up with the addition of top hitter Bob McLish who had moved over from Little's team and was considered to be the only threat to end Emerald's five-year run to the national tournament. There would be seven teams in the league, with Horton's, Foremost, United Machinery, Frosts and Har-Bell Sporting Goods, joining the fray but all were generally considered to be also-rans. The Har-Bell team was a combination of some of last year's Hamlin team and South Street Christian, which had been dominate in a church league and had nearly upset AAA champ Gaslight Realty in the city tournament behind the pitching of knuckleballer Don McDaniel.

Our Horton's club had a general distaste for the big money teams Emerald and News and Leader. We had developed instant rivalries with Foremost after we had scammed them of the best defensive catcher in the league in Mark Gann and shortstop Steve

Hutton and Har-Bell after the Hamlin team split up. The newspaper didn't realize what they had lost in seldom used and greatly under-appreciated second baseman Jim "Spare" March. We began the season with a lot of players with chips on their shoulders adding to their already competitive nature. We fought tooth and nail every game and in our opening game we defeated Har-Bell 2-1 in extra innings when "Spare" rifled a line drive through the middle to drive in the winning run. The Horton's team continued undefeated and then it came time to face off with Emerald Finance in a game where most folks nodded in agreement that we would get our comeuppance. Not bothering to have Burlison come in from Tulsa for the game, Little would throw reliable Gary McDaniel against us, taking our team a little too lightly. Gary Mac threw a good game, allowing only one run, with Jim March blasting an inside the park home run in the fourth inning. But that proved to be enough as Steve Hutton leaned over the fence down the third base line to snag Sammy Potter's popup for the last out. We had more problems with the good hitting News and Leader club. We were intentionally walking Wayne Ryan with runners on second and third when I got the pitch too close to the plate and Wayne slammed it off the left field wall driving in both runs and sealing the victory. With Steve Stewart still at University of Missouri, Jim Horton decided to throw himself against a pretty potent Frost's team. We lost 4-3 with shortstop Steve Long homering over the left field fence.

For our next meeting with Emerald, manager Jim Little made sure Burlison would be on hand to avenge their only loss, thus far, of the first half. I couldn't dream of a more enticing scenario to play out. I would be pitching against possibly the best pitcher in the world on one of the top two or three teams in the nation in the prime 7:20 p.m. time slot at Fassnight Park. It was dusk as we started warming up and I was intently going about my business when Gus Henry, playfully warming up underhanded with Rod Towe, let one get away and smacked me in the side of the head. At first I was irate, but Gus just laughed, taking away my nervousness and eliminating the edge everyone was experiencing. I took the mound grappling as usual with the extra adrenalin coursing through my body and began focusing on "Scrapper's" directions.

I had developed a low-rise ball over the past few years partially due to my having to let up to control my overzealousness early in ball games. I threw to Larry Hale as usual as the first and third basemen played him tight at the corners in hopes of taking away the bunt. A low rise to the outside corner for a strike, a drop just outside for a ball, another low rise for a strike and then a high rise, up and in, to jam him. Gann and I used this routine against almost all lefthanded hitters and Emerald had a lot of them. Mixed in with a changeup occasionally, this method proved to be successful time after time. I had watched Little's teams wreck havoc over the years against a lot of clubs using bunts and aggressive base running to completely destroy defenses, sometimes scoring four or five runs an inning with the ball never leaving the infield unless an infielder tossed one away. Our stellar defense, with our infielders following fundamentals and being exceptionally quick, made that impossible.

Burlison was quickly introduced to the Horton's team in the first inning as Mike Brooks led off with a walk, Tommy Smith followed up with a slicing hit over Larry Hale's head at first, and Rod Towe drove them both in with a double into the left center field gap. We added another run later in the game, but it was more than enough as Emerald pushed only one run across the plate. I was "in the groove", as the old saying goes, totally focused on the next pitch to the next batter. As I waited on the bench to throw the next inning I didn't want to talk to anyone, my mind narrowed to the task at hand. The exception was catcher Mark Gann, who never seemed overly excited about anything just enjoying the game. As we were getting ready for the last inning I asked "Scrapper" what we should do when facing the heart of their order the next inning. Mark just smiled and said, "Don't worry about it, Danny I've got'em right here," as he pointed to the palm of his hand. I walked to the end of the bench and stepped behind the fence. I reached into my warmup jacket and pulled out a pack of cigarettes. Lighting up a Winston I allowed myself to relax and pull my thoughts together, which meant disposing of them. I walked back out to the mound and refocused. No negative thoughts, no images of celebration, not thinking, only throwing, just me and "Scrapper" carving up the middle of the lineup. Mark had been right. We had topped the best thrower in the world 3-1 handing him his first league loss in the two years he had spent here. I was ecstatic!! It was the highlight of my career. I would pitch a few better games but none ever meant as much to me.

The newspaper team would hand us another loss but also defeated Emerald in their second meeting, so the first half ended with Horton's and Emerald in a first-place tie. Over the summer we played some good ball in tournaments. We finished second to a really good Oran, Missouri, team that featured John Watkins on the mound at Poplar Bluff. With losses to Larry Sparks of Jeff City Mid-State Oil and Bob Thornton of Decatur, Illinois, in the Jefferson City tournament, we managed a third-place finish. Among our wins was a 3-2 victory over defending state titlist Jeff City Rippeto Carpet. We won tournaments in West Plains, defeating Har-Bell in the finals and besting them again at the Fox Hollow championship game. Both times they had blown through the loser's bracket and forced an extra game by beating us in the first game of the double elimination finals. The West Plains final was highlighted by "Stump" Stombaugh's inside the park homerun in the first inning against me. The center field fence was over 400 feet away. "Stump" lined a pitch over Gus Henry's head in center and the speedy runner had rounded the bases and was sitting on the bench when Gus finally chased it down and got it back into the infield. He never let me forget that one. We were fortunate in the last innings as; with one out and the winning runs on second and third. Rick Jackson shot a line drive down the third base line only to be snagged by Gary Stracke who stepped on the base for a game ending double play. Outfielder Jim Logan had 12 hits in 20 trips to the plate batting a lofty .600 for the tournament. The Horton's team also won an after-season tournament in Lebanon, Missouri with pickup player Rondell Miller selected Most Valuable Player.

The second half of the league play was not as successful for us. We split two games with News and Leader, lost twice to Har-Bell, the second being shut out by Jerry Mallonee in a 3-0 loss. After losing to Emerald 5-2 the first time around we rebounded in the second game to beat them 7-0. We had defeated the favorites three out of four and in those three wins they had scored only one time. They routed our team 7-2 in the first half playoff game and beat Har-Bell in the other game to successfully defend their sixth straight league title. District time was at hand.

Joplin Tri-State Tournament
Danny Miles pitching against Emerald Finance of Springfield, and their star pitcher Roy Burlison.

# Seventeen

## The Rat in the Hat

The '75 season brought forth some new talent up from the open leagues. United Machinery was a very young team and showcased new pitchers Tim Baker and Steve Hanson. Steve was the nephew of pitcher/manager/sponsor Al Hanson. Tim was the brother of my Hamlin teammate Steve Baker. Their father, Paul, had a walk route with the post office but never walked. He jogged and sprinted his route every day then came home and caught Tim every evening as he learned to pitch. Steve worked with good friend and teammate Jim Logan in the sports department at Kmart where they often rolled up their pant legs and performed "We are the Lollipop Guild" from the Wizard of Oz. Along with the two throwers were players of note third baseman Stu Dunlop and catcher Rondell Miller. John Carr pitched for Frost's and came around in the second half to throw some good games, and multi-talented Randy Johnson showed a lot of promise at several different positions. The newcomer to make the biggest impression was hurler Jerry Mallonee who ended the season with an 8-5 record doing mound duty for Har-Bell. He had shutout Emerald Finance in a second half game before beating us 3-0.

We started the district by topping an open league team 3-1

behind Steve Stewart and faced off against Foremost for a state berth. Rod Towe and Mark Gann were in the National Guard and were required to attend camp at Fort Hood, Texas, that same week. Being innovative, they caught a ride home on an army helicopter returning to Springfield in time to play the Foremost game. I started the game matched against pitcher Shelby Hill. Foremost jumped to a lead and going into the fifth inning we were trailing 4-1. That brought in Steve Stewart to relieve and he shut them out the rest of the game. In the sixth, we scored two runs to trail by just one and had a runner on first base and Tommy Smith, the tying run, on second with two outs. The catcher caught Tommy napping and picked him cleanly off base. In the ensuing run down Foremost mishandled a throw and Tom ended up scoring the tying run. We added three runs in the seventh to win 7-4 and qualify for the state tournament. Our luck didn't hold out.

Rod and Mark, driving all night back to Fort Hood in Mark's girlfriend's Volkswagen bug, came up about 30 miles short when the car broke down and they didn't make inspection the next morning. The punishment could have been worse as they both forfeited their pay but escaped further disciplinary action. Unfortunately, they missed the winners' bracket finals when we played the newspaper team. Jim Horton started the game but, even with relief help from Steve Stewart, we lost. Stewart pitched the next game topping Foremost 3-1 backed by Steve Hutton's three-run homer. We played News and Leader club again and with the game tied 0-0 after six innings they pushed across three runs in the top of the seventh. We responded with two in the bottom of the inning but that wasn't enough as Steve Murdaugh threw another great game against us. We had guaranteed ourselves a spot in the state tournament thanks mainly to the clutch pitching of Stewart, some timely hitting, and a little luck. Horton relished watching the loser's bracket games after we had qualified to, as he zealously emphasized, "watch the eliminations"!

The Har-Bell team had failed to earn a spot in the state so we picked up pitcher Jerry Mallonee and center fielder Jim Dopp for the tournament. Dopp was a solid hitter with power and a good outfielder with a sense of humor as we found out as he related an incident with Har-Bell's manager Don McDaniel. Dopp was playing center field one night when he dropped an easy fly ball allowing a couple of runs to score. McDaniel called timeout, grabbed a glove off the bench and trotted out to center and had Jim switch mitts, adding insult to injury. Mallonee was quick to bestow nicknames on his fellow teammates, like "Bozo" for Richie Gleghorn based on his somewhat bulbous nose and "Tree" for large catcher Rod Jones. Steve Stombaugh had named knuckle ball thrower Don McDaniel "McThumber" and his everpresent bulldog "McThumbPup". Dopp had christened Jerry "the Rat in the Hat", which we all shortened to "Rat", a moniker he was stuck with by competitors and teammates throughout his career.

The Horton's team started the state tournament with an easy opening night win against Sedalia as Gary Stracke blasted a home run to left field. We then escaped a couple of nail biters, defeating Hannibal 9-3 in 10 innings and Marshfield 6-5 with the help of three unearned runs in the sixth. In the Hannibal game we were tied going into 10th with Gus Henry in the -deck circle and runners in scoring position. Hannibal decided to make a pitching change and during warm ups manager Horton went over to discuss the situation with Gus. As he walked back to the third base coaching box Gus's dad Denny stepped to the fence to add some instruction. Then former player and coach Bill Knight motioned for Gus to join him as he added his two cents worth. With that, Gus turned to the crowd and asked in a loud voice "Does anyone else want to tell me how to hit?" We ended up with a six-run inning to put the game out of reach.

Between those ball games several of us had retired to the Dugout to relive our victories over a couple of beers when Denny Henry came over to the table and advised us, "You can't win the tournament in here!", causing us to shortcut our celebration. Steve Stewart pitched the first game the next day as we beat Jefferson City Midstate Oil 4-3, putting us into the winners' bracket semifinal against twice defending champion Jeff City Rippeto. The champs got to me early in the game and, behind the pitching of John Watkins, defeated us 5-1, putting us up against a good Joplin team. Jerry Mallonee took the mound and we topped them 7-4. We would now be facing News and Leader and our old nemesis and good friend, hurler Steve Murdaugh. Stewart threw six strong shutout innings but ran into trouble in the bottom of the sixth. I relieved with runners on second and third and two outs with us up

3-2. I got two strikes on catcher Donnie Haworth but couldn't get that third one by him. After pulling several rise balls foul down the third base line I decided to let up just a little on the next one hoping for a popup. It is the pitch I would most have liked to have back in my career as he bounced a hit between short and third driving in the winning runs and giving us a fourth-place finish. The newspaper team lost to Jeff City Rippeto in the losers' finals before St. Joseph Walnut Products pounded the defending champs 10-0 in the finals. It would be the first of several state tournament championships for the St. Joe squad. At the beginning of the year few would have predicted our strong league and state play, but we knew we had a chance to be a great team.

1979 St. Joseph Walnut Products

Front row: Ed Smith, Wayne Miller, Roger Smith, Charlie Pusateri, Charlie Blakley, Bob Holt, Paul Lemon, Leo Blakley

Back row: Ken Christgen, Sr., HL Childress, Jerry McDaniel, Herb Lucas, Larry Sparks, Kirby Hatcher, Mike Bray, Tim O'Brien

With the onset of slow pitch play in town the number of fast pitch teams had been dwindling steadily, but the AAA crowds had held up at Fassnight Park giving us a great atmosphere in which to perform. The level of competition was still strong in town and on the road. The number of teams fell, but those that endured were stronger with the best players having fewer options of where to play. We had finished second in the league and finished 6-2 in the state meet showing ourselves to be one of the best teams in the Midwest. The "hot stove" league would be heating up soon as all thoughts turned to next year.

# THE BIG SIX

The pitchers that dominated ASA national tournaments from the 1960's until the 1980's.

Ty Stofflet

Weldon Haney

Roy Burlison

Joe Lynch

DANNY MILES

Bonnie Jones

Harvey Sterkel

# Eighteen

## The Spirit of '76

The 1975 season had seen a changing of the guard in the women's hierarchy as perennial powerhouses. North Missouri CTs and defending state champion Springfield Foremost had been defeated in state play by Springfield's Big Blue. While Foremost still carried big names like hurler Cindy Henderson, Sue Murdaugh, Jackie Tekotte and Carol Myers, they had been upstaged by a team of basically high school girls coached by Foremost player Sue Murdaugh. Big Blue featured top pitcher Penny Clayton who joined players Mary and Joanie French, Jean Eubanks, Elaine Fields, Cathy Bishop, and smooth swinging Lisa Nicholson in forming a strong Southwest Missouri State nucleus for several years to come. Cindy Henderson and Carol Myers would star the next few years with Detroit in the International Professional Women's League.

Emerald Finance had won their fifth regional beating Clear Lake, Iowa, in the finals at St. Louis. They had picked up Wayne Ryan from the newspaper and Rod Towe from our team and those proved to be valuable assets as they led Emerald in offense for the tournament. The team was upset in the opening round, losing to Atlanta, Georgia, before rebounding with wins against defending champ Santa Rosa, California, 2-1 with Towe throwing out the winning run in the seventh inning. Oklahoma City was blanked by Burleson 3-0 before they were slammed by Detroit, Michigan, and big lefty Edmore Johnson 7-0, ending with a seventh-place finish. First baseman Larry Hale set a record by reaching base his first 11 times at the plate and was named to the all-tournament team. It was Emerald's sixth straight national tournament appearance.

Over the winter manager Jim Horton had wrangled the sponsorship from News and Leader. We had the good fortune of adding their top thrower Steve Murdaugh and hitsman Wayne Ryan. With those two additions everything looked good for a run at the league championship and the state title to be played in St. Joseph. Three really good pitchers had rejoined the AAA ranks as Kenny Williams played for CMI (formerly Emerald Finance), Tim Buff came off the injured list to join Foremost, and Phil Wilkerson was added to the Frost's team after a three-year absence from the league. Most of the Frost's team would be made up of last year's News and Leader team. Also in the league would be Har-Bell, McDonald's and The Bottlers, a team spun off of last season's United Machinery team. Larry Marshall reentered the league throwing for McDonald's and flashed some signs of old, pitching several good games and tossing a two-hit shutout against us.

Frost's made it clear early they would be a serious contender as Phil Wilkerson beat Roy Burlison in their opening game with CMI. It was only the second loss for Burleson in three years of league play. Our News and Leader team had a great start topping CMI in our first two meetings 5-2 and 8-5 before tripping up against The Bottlers and losing one to Frost's. We swept through an early tournament in Poplar Bluff defeating Oran, Missouri, in the finals with Murdaugh on the mound. In honor of the nation's bicentennial celebration Falstaff brewery launched a special can commemorating the event and we downed several cases over the summer in patriotic observance.

Next came the strong Jefferson City meet where we finished third even though Murdaugh had shut out repeat champion Decataur, Illinois, 1-0. The league became a three-team race with CMI taking the title to our second-place finish and a close third by Frost's. Tommy Smith hit over .400 in the league, with Wayne Ryan, Rod Towe, Jim March and Steve Murdaugh all batting above .300 for the year. Manager Jerry Burwell and Ancil Fry had pulled together a good Foremost team that jelled during the district to win the tournament over Frost's and our News and Leader team, with all three qualifying for the state meet. Tim Buff had returned to top form and the addition of left-hander Earl Rivers had pushed Foremost to the top with the help of a healthy Jim McDaniel at the plate. Jim Smith, Steve Hutchinson, Don Henderson, Bill Helfrect and catcher Jim Nichols added to their now potent offense. The Foremost club always seemed to struggle during the season but managed to get to the state tournament year after year.

Steve Stewart got us off to a good start in St. Joseph no-hitting Willow Springs in five innings. Next up was Pacific with former Springfieldian Sterling Price on the mound. We had lost to Price during the summer as a pickup player pitching for St. Louis Kutis. That afternoon game followed a memorable team get together known forever as the "Du Wa Ditty" party. The party was hosted by roommates Gus Henry, Jim Hamilton and Kevin Hughes. After a lot of alcohol consumption Gus was playing a tape of Western Swing music by Commander Cody and the Lost Planet Airmen. One of the songs, a remake of a song called "That's What I Like About The South" originally done by Phil Harris, got more and more play as the night wore on. As the song got louder different players seemed obliged to take to the dance floor for some solo performances that became more and more hilarious. Finally, Gus stripped off his shirt and donned a white apron challenging anyone to wrestle "Butcher Boy" Henry. I don't think there were any takers. One line of the song was, "There's a place called Du Wa Ditty, it aint a town and it aint a city, say Du Wa Ditty," which gave the party its title. Price had been the beneficiary of our team-wide hangover in that game but we slammed him with six runs in the first and four in the second inning, including home runs by Wayne Ryan and Rod Towe. I did not do my part as I was pulled for relief help from Murdaugh in the second inning, leaving with three runs on the board and the bases loaded. We won that game in five innings only to lose to St Joe's Walnut Products 4-1 in eight innings. We had left the winning run on third in the last inning when Ryan missed a sign and couldn't score on a fly ball with one out. Our chances to get back to the title game were slim but the next morning started with optimism.

The day started with a game against Fairport ending in a 5-2 win. The park had several shade trees behind the outfield fence. As the sun rose so did the temperature and the shade in center field kept shrinking toward the fence. I noticed from the mound that centerfielder Gus Henry kept playing deeper and deeper keeping in the shade. By the end of the game Gus was practically leaning against the barrier. I kidded him about it after the game and he replied, "I come in on the ball really well!" I had an eight-track tape of "Doc" Watson songs, including "Southbound Passenger Train". With Tom Smith, brother Jim, and Rod Towe in the car we adopted that song as our good luck charm and played it on every trip back and forth from the ballpark. It worked well the rest of the day. Murdaugh beat a St. Joe team and pitcher Robert Sublett and Stewart followed suit with a late win against Sedalia as Rod Towe hit an inside-the-park home run in the last inning. We faced the final day having to win six straight games to claim the championship. A difficult chore but we had Wayne Ryan and Steve Murdaugh to give us a chance.

Sunday morning saw us facing Maryville and good pitcher Duane Huff, but I had a good game and shut them out winning 4-0. It was decided that I would start again the next game against Oran and John Watkins. It turned out to be a bad decision as I left in the first inning behind 3-0 after watching a home run disappear over the wall at Walnut Park. "Murt" came on and shut them out the rest of the game as we scrambled to get back into the game. With Mike Brooks on first and two outs in the bottom of the seventh, Tom Smith was our last chance. Watkins threw and Tommy popped up weakly right at the plate. Amazingly, the Oran catcher dropped the ball keeping our hopes alive. Tommy then grounded a ball between first and second, which bounced off Brooksy's leg as he ran to second into the outfield. It looked like our season was over with what we assumed would be an interference call but umpire Bob Jackson (from Springfield) ruled that the ball could have been fielded by the first baseman so there was no interference. Rod Towe followed with a base hit to score the tying run. After going into extra innings Ryan ended the game with a homer over the left centerfield fence. Definitely a lucky win.

Next up was our hometown competitor Frost's. With Phil Wilkerson and Steve Murdaugh locked in a 1-1 contest, Frost's

Randy Johnson was on first base with two outs late in the game when Mike Egly lined a shot toward right center. Jim Logan cut the ball off before it got to the fence and made a perfect cut-off throw to second baseman Jim March who turned and hit catcher Mark Gann with an accurate toss to nail Johnson at the plate. For the second straight game Wayne Ryan connected for a game-winning home run in the eighth inning for a 2-1 win.

We had won three in a row but now the state championship was between us and two St Joe teams. Roto-Rooter had downed defending champ Walnut Products in the winner's final so we would be facing Herb "Ironman" Lucas on the mound for Walnut in the loser's final. Walnut had a great, seasoned squad with good defense and power hitters Charley Pusitari, Mickey Cooper, Charlie Blakely, Jerry McDaniel, Leo Blakely, Roger Smith, and the Gallager brothers. The hometown fans were well into their cups of Pearl beer by late evening and loudly heckled "Murt" and catcher Mark Gann. "Scrapper" Gann had hair down to mid back and endured inning after inning of insults but would occasionally turn to the crowd after digging another Murdaugh drop ball out of the dirt and give them a big smile and waggle his glove with the ball inside. The game was tight, tied 2-2 in the last inning, when Gann bounced a hit over Jerry McDaniel's head at third driving in the winning run. During the game the Walnut coach was yelling at Lucas not to swing at pitches in the dirt when "Ironman" yelled back, "How do I know they're in the dirt until I swing at'em?" Horton decided to stay with Murdaugh whose big drop just kept getting better the more tired he became.

We took on Roto-Rooter in the first game having to win both games to win the tournament and overcoming hitters Jackie Jackson and the Hicks brothers, Al and Teddy. Al had been a great hitter for a long time and Ted was fast becoming one of the best hitters I ever watched play. We got on top early with Ryan and Murdaugh hitting solo home runs, but St. Joe came back to go ahead 3-2. Twice Horton had Murdaugh intentionally walk Jackie Jackson to load the bases with fewer than two outs and he worked out of both jams. In the last inning with the tying run on third and two outs, Jim Logan came to the plate and bounced a routine grounder to short looking like an end to the game, but "Clownie" hustled down the line and beat the throw sending the game into extra innings. In the 12th inning pitcher Jim Mears lined a double into left center to drive in the winning run giving Roto-Rooter the championship.

It was an amazing day on several fronts with most of our players playing almost nonstop for 42 innings. Jim March had the flu and spent every spare minute covered up with blankets until the next game started. "Scrapper", in probably the most exhausting of positions, caught every pitch in every inning. Ryan had slammed three home runs, two of them game winners, and played great shortstop. Steve Murdaugh had produced the greatest pitching performance I have ever witnessed throwing 35 innings that Sunday, which lasted from eight in the morning until after midnight. It was a long trip back home, with Gann falling asleep in the back of a car and not awakening until our return to Springfield. We had again fallen short of our goal, but we were getting closer.

# Nineteen

## Long Necks

It began as poor scheduling for mid-July in Missouri. Hot and humid and driving closer and closer to the Mississippi River, it was all well-intended but ill conceived. Horton's manager, Jim Horton, had us beginning the trip with a double header set for 1:00 in Flat River and then driving north for two more games that evening against St. Louis Kutis and then two more games on Sunday.

We loaded up my '68 Impala with fellow pitcher Steve Murdaugh, my brother Jim, first baseman Mike Brooks and a cooler full of beer for our 8 a.m. start. It was a long trip from Springfield to Flat River in those days on two lane roads most of the way. As the day wore on it became hotter and hotter and the air thicker and thicker. For some strange reason we allowed Murt to drive, which let him man handle the air conditioner. Being the ace of the staff and overly protective of his throwing arm, he refused to turn it on, so we managed the best we could with windows rolled down. It was tolerable at best for me riding shot gun, but the guys in the back were slow roasted in their own sweat.

We arrived at the ballpark in Flat River to find it laid out on a treeless, open plain as far as the eye could see. I am sure there was grass in the outfield but I truly do not remember seeing any. From the bench you could look out across the field and see the simmering heat rising in small spirals toward the sun-drenched skies. Jim spent most of the day following the shade of the only light pole on our side of the field in an effort to get some relief from the sun. I was fortunate that I was not penciled in to pitch either game, so the duties fell to Murdaugh and Steve Stewart. Murt was a drop ball pitcher and a really good one. The more he tired the better his ball broke, and drop ball throwers are consistent in either daylight or darkness. The first game was an easy win for us, but the second not so much. Stewart depended a lot on his rise ball although he had a good drop and changeup. He was a control pitcher who blended in all three pitches to get the job done.

Steve attended law school at Missouri University and had a large head full of brains. He also possessed a large booming voice and a big, competitive heart matched only by the size of his balls. He was never afraid to go right after the very best of hitters and won most of those battles. Unfortunately, weather and the amount of light affects rise ballers to a great extent. Humidity resists the reverse rotation on the ball making it a fairly flat pitch, plus it is much easier to pick up in the daytime. In these kinds of conditions location becomes of the utmost importance, and Steve was always up to that task. It wasn't a pretty win but a win none the less. We reloaded the cars for the two-hour drive to St. Louis.

Pevely Softball Complex was built to accommodate the many slow pitch teams in the St. Louis area so the fences were at 275 feet instead of the regulation 250. The fields were placed in a semi-circle under a fairly good-sized hill. The concession stand was at the top of the hill with a somewhat steep dirt path leading to it. The heat and the mugginess continued to drain us and I had a very poor outing on the mound. Not possessing Stewart's drop ball or his pinpoint control, my rise balls continually curved to the middle of the plate instead of going up, and the powerful Kutis team pounded out a lot of line drives. I could often get ahead in the count to second baseman Bobby Robin, but it seemed he always managed a two-strike hit. Outfielder Ray Rohr was a power hitter and I can't ever remember pitching a game against him when he didn't end up parking one over the left field fence. This game was no exception. After a few innings Stewart was called on to relieve with better success, but the damage had been done. They had positioned some sawhorses at 250 feet at various places around the outfield to serve as home run or ground rule double barriers. Murdaugh threw a good second game, but Rohr caught up with a big drop with two runners on sending it far into the night. Horton ran out to argue the umpire's call of a home run, but Murdaugh cut him off saying, "That one was well out", thus ending that discussion.

During the second game our centerfielder, Gus Henry, cramped up after trying to beat out an infield grounder. Gus was on his fourth game of the day, had consumed a good amount of beer on the trip and was dehydrated. The ever scholarly and even more frugal Brooks instantly sized up the problem and stated, as Gus grimaced in pain on the base path, "Give me a quarter, Gus, and I will get you a coke."

The Kutis manager was Norb Thurmer who was the proprietor of Thurmer's Bar located at the corner of Chippewa and Virginia in the old Dutchtown neighborhood in south St. Louis. He invited us to the bar after the game. I was at first reluctant as I did not want to patronize with anyone who had just pounded us for two games, but we loaded up a couple of cars with six or eight sweaty, nasty ballplayers wearing the uniforms they had worn since eight o'clock that morning and headed to the bar.

If my memory is correct the bar was fairly narrow and long fitting the lot. Most of the neighborhood houses mirrored this configuration of "shotgun housing" representative of many older cities. As we pulled up to the corner, we noticed some beer trucks bringing in two-wheeler loads of beer of every variety. Gravel voiced Kenny Heck, Kutis third base coach, explained that most of Thurmer's income came from Sunday sales. Somehow in the past the bar had grabbed a Sunday beer license and was one of the few places in beer guzzling St. Louis where it was available. At this time the only place in the whole city that had higher beer sales was Busch Stadium. People lined up around the block to carry out case after case because drinking inside the bar was apparently against the law on the Sabbath. The old bar showed its age with heavy wooden tables and chairs, hardwood floors, and some well-worn beer signs. A little on the dingy side, it was comfortable and inviting to those who enjoyed socializing and sharing a few stories with their brew. It was definitely my kind of atmosphere. Thurmer disappeared into the small kitchen and threw on some good sized ribeyes and baked potatoes. He informed us that everything was on the house and we readily agreed to the invitation. The steaks were really good, especially when you consider that we had hardly eaten all day, but not nearly as good as the beer.

 I drank a lot of beer in those days and my choice was Busch. I ordered, expecting a can or a glass from the tap, but I was pleasantly surprised. Busch was a product from Anheuser-Busch that had been developed in the '50s to appeal to women. It was much lighter and sweeter than the strong and grainy Budweiser which, I believe, remains the largest selling beer in the United States. The beer was served in long-necked glass bottles, which still had a thin film of ice on the exterior. The moisture ran down your fingers as you picked the bottle up, and the beer was clean and crisp flowing into your throat. After a good meal and lots of stories and cold ones the tribulations of the day turned into an evening well spent. We stayed until the bar had to close and Norb followed us outside with a case of Bud. We sat on the brick sidewalk on the curb outside the bar and exchanged pleasantries with the neighborhood policemen that drove by. Unlike Springfield, it was not against the law to consume alcohol on the street. To say we slept well that night would be a no-brainer and we bounced up the next day only to lose two more games before slinking back to the Ozarks. Best beer I ever had.

# Twenty

## On the Road Again

I enjoyed road trips although not all players did. I loved the camaraderie and the competition with teams from throughout the Midwest. Most trips included four guys to a room, irregular and unhealthy meals, coarse language, and over consumption of alcohol. If possible, we might get our uniforms laundered after play on Saturday, usually depending upon the presence of Gus Henry's mother, Anita. Duke, Gus's dad, and Anita made almost every road trip, dragging their three daughters along with them. Steve Hutton often lamented that it took him two weeks to recover from the ill effects of playing out of town. He would have to clean up his language and regulate his bowel movements. By that time, we were usually back on the road.

Jefferson City was an oft-visited city and most teams either stayed at the tall cylindrical Capitol Inn downtown or the sprawling Ramada Inn on Highway 54. The advantage of the Ramada was that it sat on a hill overlooking the highway and down the slope on the opposite side of the road was Oscar's Steakhouse. The restaurant was spacious featuring a full bar and some great steaks. Every team playing in a tournament there ended up, sooner or later, having a meal at Oscar's. Our Hamlin team had made its way to the restaurant, scrambling down the two steep slopes and dodging traffic on the busy highway. After dinner and several drinks some of the players began the somewhat treacherous journey back up the hill. With that group was Mike Wolfe's father, Arnie, who had downed quite a few cocktails before the trek. A few of us were still in the restaurant when "Stump" Stombaugh took notice of the situation and offered a five-dollar bet to any takers that Arnie wouldn't make it up the hill without falling. Arnie was just ready to take the final steps when he slipped and slid some distance from the highway. "Stump" laughed merrily as he collected the wagers. Jim Radar and Steve Murdaugh made use of the large Ramada parking lot by challenging each other to a streaking race late one night. After a rapid trip around the parking lot they both ended up pounding on the motel room door as Harold Harris took his sweet time unlocking it for the bare-naked racers.

Wayne Ryan was known to over consume some beer upon occasion. On one trip to Jeff City he somehow managed to commandeer the Indianapolis, Indiana, team bus. He, with the help of brothers Gus and Joe Henry, abandoned the vehicle on the steps of the state capitol building. As one of the Indianapolis players was telling us the story of their "borrowed" bus we could hear Wayne snickering in the background. After another late night of partying Wayne and a group were out driving around the city when Wayne needed to take a leak. They pulled over to the curb and Wayne urinated on a large sign. As he scrambled back into the car he asked, "What does JCPD" stand for? The answer as they sped off was, "Jefferson City Police Department!"

Teddy West could become loud and somewhat obnoxious when drinking and didn't mind if a few fisticuffs ensued. One night he was challenged in a bar and responded, "I would rather fight and lose than not get to fight!" This time was a loss and one of his teammates asked him what had happened. Ted said that he knew he was in trouble when the guy crawled out of the booth and he saw that he had a life-size tattoo of a tiger on his bicep! At breakfast one morning during the Joplin tournament someone asked Ted how he was doing after a night of heavy drinking. He replied, "I sat down on the stool this morning and it felt like a covey of blackbirds flew out of my rear end!"

During the Columbia tournament a couple of the News and

Leader players had gone out on the town and wound up going skinny dipping with two ladies they had connected with at a nearby bar. As they climbed out of the "swimming pool" they noticed a sign that read City of Columbia Wastewater Treatment Plant. They hurried back to the motel for a long shower. Two of the Scenic Shopper team had taken off after their last game of the day. They returned to the motel about eight o'clock the next morning still wearing their uniforms. Their wives had driven up that morning and were in the lobby as the two walked in the front door. One looked at his wife and said, "We were just going to breakfast." I am not sure the girls bought that story.

Our News and Leader team was entered in the Topeka tournament and manager Jim Horton had obtained tickets for a Kansas City Royals game we could attend on the way up. Jim March and Steve Hutton were going to make the trip with Mike Brooks who told them he would pick them up at two that afternoon at the News and Leader office where they worked. They both begged their way into getting off a couple of hours early and they waited for Brooksy in the parking lot. They waited impatiently for two hours sitting in the lot with their bags packed until 4 o'clock when the rest of the office workers streamed out of the building and waved goodbye to them on their way home. Mike finally showed up and proceeded to drive his new car at 55 miles per hour all the way to Kansas City, not trying to make up any time. When Jim March asked him to turn the air conditioning on he replied he wasn't using it to obtain better fuel economy. When they arrived at the park Brooksy bounced out of the car and sprinted to the gate to get the tickets. Hutton looked at March and said, "Look who's in a hurry all of a sudden."

Jim Logan came up late to a meet in Jeff City and had partied late after arriving. I woke him the next morning and asked him, "How's the old bulldog this morning?" He looked up with squinting eyes and told me how he awoke early and opened his eyes to see Brooksy sitting in the wide-open bathroom with a bowel movement grimace on his face. "Clownie" said he groaned and rolled over and thought, "This is going to be one hell of a day." Mike's best performance was before a full house in our Jeff City motel room. With most of the team on hand lounging between games a couple of the guys were lying at the foot of the bed watching TV. Mike came out of the shower completely nude and walked over to the television. He bent over and started changing the channel with his rear end just inches from two of the players' faces. They simultaneously rolled off the sides of the bed to escape the spectacle. We were never sure if those were examples of Mike's unusual sense of humor or just his gross behavior. I have always hoped the former.

After a weekend tournament in St. Louis Steve Stewart hopped into a car and was dropped off at his house by teammates. When he came into the house his wife Krissy asked simply, "Where's the car?" Steve had left the Volvo sitting in the motel parking lot. He maintains that it was a miscommunication between him and Mark Gann, who had asked to take the car home early but then made other arrangements. Anyway, that's Steve's story.

# Twenty-One

## "Rat" - Trap

Once again Jim Little's CMI team had won the regional tournament by topping state champion Roto Rooter in the finals. They finished the nationals with a 2-2 record knocking off Clearwater 2-1 and a very good Seattle team 4-1. They dropped games to Sunnyvale, California, and 1-0 to left hander Ty Stofflet and Reading, Pennsylvania, on the way to a seventh-place finish. One of the highlights of the '76 season was a visit from Reading for two exhibition games, one against CMI and one against our newspaper team. We faced off against tall thrower Larry Berg. Jim Horton had planned to let each of our three throwers pitch two or three innings but at the end of the 3$^{rd}$ starter Steve Murdaugh was holding the defending national champs hitless and without a run. Steve Stewart and I urged Horton to keep Murt in the game. He and Berg matched two hitters with Reading winning in the eighth on a solo home run by their catcher. Stofflet topped CMI and Roy Burlison 2-0 in the final game with two bunt singles by Joe Henry being the only base runners for CMI. Between the three teams there were a total of nine base hits allowed in the 15 innings played.

Over 1,500 fans had jammed into Fassnight Park to watch fast pitch softball at its best. The week before the exhibition games the park board had installed a snow fence in the outfield to move the distance back to 250 feet. Our game was tight and Murdaugh was to warm up for possible relief. It was Steve Hutton's turn to sit out so the duty of warming up Murt fell to him. They started behind the first base fence and every time Hut mishandled one of Murt's drops in the dirt he walked to retrieve it only to find Murt had hustled up to hurry his heating up. After several times of this recurrence Murt was called in to the game but he entered from the third base side behind the other team's bench. Little's teams had won seven league titles in a row, won one state, six regionals, and played in seven consecutive national tournaments. If that wasn't enough, over the winter they had recruited Murdaugh to join them for the '77 season leaving us to scramble for another pitcher. We had split the league contests with them and it had taken a no hitter from Burlison to defeat Steve Stewart 2-1 to get them even. The newspaper had withdrawn their sponsorship and in addition we had lost two of our best hitters. Wayne Ryan went to play with Foremost and Tommy Smith signed on with CMI.

Just as we seemed ready to make a major breakthrough as a team we were again thwarted in our attempts. Horton had managed to come up with enough money to get things started and we went back to being called Horton's, added versatile players Randy Johnson and Joe Henry, and after much debate and insistence from Stewart and myself we offered the third pitcher job to young and unproven Lonnie Marshall. Lonnie had light red hair and freckles reminding us of the descriptions of Huckleberry Finn. We tried to stick that nickname on him but it didn't adhere. He was only unproven at the AAA level — his team had won the Young Men's State Tournament and finished second in the national championship. Lonnie was the oldest son of former AAA pitcher Larry Marshall and possessed all the "stuff" needed to make a good thrower. All he needed was a good defense and a great catcher. With Mark Gann behind the plate we could deliver all the necessities. With Stewart still at law school for a couple of weeks Lonnie would be tested quickly. The additions of Johnson and Joe Henry didn't hurt us at all defensively but our offense would be in question.

The 1977 AAA league was the strongest it had been in several years. CMI was the odds- on favorite to dominate the circuit with a great hitting team featuring the likes of Larry Hale, Beau Robinson, Jerry Burnett, Jim Maggi, Kelly Whitaker and Tommy Smith. Bonus Frost would play later in the year as would Kelly Burre and Larry Earlywine from Jefferson City. Marshfield Mill could throw pitchers Kenny Williams, Jim Collins and Phil Wilkerson at you with the good offense of Kenny Brown, Jim Rader, Ron Crosswhite, Mike Egly, Harold Harris and Sammy Potter. Har-Bell would be managed by Mike Larmer and added Randy Towe, Mike McTeer and Larry Plaster to an already solid team. Jim Dopp, Larry Cotter, Gary Palmer, the Gleghorn brothers, Bobby and Richie, were already established players in the league. Jerry "Rat" Mallonee and Gary Augustine would be on the mound. Foremost had built the strongest contender it would field in the last few years. Pitchers Tim Buff, Earl Rivers and Lige Williams, combined with hitters Wayne Ryan, Steve Hutchinson, Jim McDaniel, Jim Nichols, Bill Helfrect, Ancil Fry and Donnie Henderson, completed a formidable line up. A new entry in the league under the sponsorship of Northern Lights Ice had assembled a competitive club. With young pitchers John Carr and Steve Hanson on staff they added Louie Bunch who would lead the team in hitting with a .343 average and home runs with four. Alan Potts, John Maritt, Dave McBeath, Ron Ghan and Rondell Miller gave them good depth.

 We lost our first two games out of the gate losing to Murdaugh and CMI 6-5 when former teammate Tommy Smith singled in the winning run in the seventh inning and to Marshfield and Phil Wilkerson in Lonnie's debut. We had taken second-place in an early tournament in Marshfield. One of the highlights happened during one of my plate appearances. Ronnie Crosswhite was umping behind the plate and I turned to him and said, "They had better back up Cross. I've been working out." On the first pitch I launched a drive over the centerfielder's head. The field didn't have fences, abutting the fairgrounds. As I ran the bases the ball rolled into one of the cattle barns. The outfielder chased it into the shed and tossed it back in, throwing from inside the building. The relay came in and I had to settle for a triple. Coach Horton was doubled over with laughter as he held me at third, amazed at my lack of speed. I lost a pitching duel with Roy Burleson 2-0 in our next match with CMI. Tommy Smith hurt us again with a solo home run over the centerfield fence, one of their two hits. They easily won the first half over second-place Marshfield, with our Horton's squad another game back.

Lonnie was getting better every game he threw and would soon be throwing even more. In mid-June, in a game against Marshfield, I was attempting to score from second on Joe Henry's double to left. I went in standing up with the ball close behind. Catcher Junior Williams tried to tag me as I crossed the plate and caught my back leg with the glove. I was flipped head over heels landing on my right shoulder. I couldn't pitch for another two weeks and had constant discomfort in my arm for several years. We were back to two throwers, meaning Lonnie and Steve Stewart each got more work. About the time I was able to pitch again Stewart went back to Missouri University to study for his upcoming bar exams, maintaining our two-pitcher rotation. We played CMI three times in the second half, beating them twice with Lonnie throwing one game and relieving me in the second.

The second half was closer, with us trailing CMI by one game going into the last night of makeup games. The first three games went as expected and we won our game, so it all came down to a game between CMI and Har-Bell. According to Jerry Mallonee, manager Jim Little tried to get Har-Bell to forfeit the game since it would be very late getting over. "Rat" said, "I tell you what, Jim. Give us $50 bucks and we'll forfeit and go down to your bar and spend it all on beer." Little declined the offer and they faced off for the last regular season contest. CMI jumped on Mallonee for six runs in the first inning. Their best hitter, Beau Robinson, had to arise early for his job with the telephone company so he headed home. A few of the Horton's team also gave up and went to the Dugout Lounge to have a beer or two. Har-Bell pecked away at the lead and tied it 6-6 in the seventh inning. Jim Logan had hung around to watch the game and came flying into the bar announcing the game was tied. We hurried to the park to watch the extra innings. In the bottom of the 13th inning Randy Towe lined a single to left that eluded outfielder Jerry Burnett and flew around the bases scoring the winning run. The "Rat" must have been pissed off by Little's rejection of his counter offer. Over the last 12 innings he allowed only three hits and for the last seven didn't allow any. We were ecstatic! Now we would play CMI a playoff game for the second half title. Winning that we would battle for the league title they had held for the last seven years.

# Twenty-Two

## Lon Juan

The Horton's squad faced a daunting task, having to defeat CMI twice in one night with Roy Burlison on the mound. CMI scored one run off pitcher Lonnie Marshall in the third, but we bounced back in the fourth with three runs. Randy Johnson had supplied the big hit with a triple to the wall scoring Mike Brooks who had walked and Rod Towe having reached on an infield hit. Johnson scored on a passed ball. Lonnie was masterful, allowing only four hits for the game as we added another run in the fifth to earn a 4-1 win. Steve Stewart was dominant in the title game, spacing out three hits over 5 1/3 innings. Steve Hutton doubled in Gus Henry and Randy Johnson following singles by both, with Hutton scoring on an error by CMI's Kelly Burre. The defending champs tied it in the sixth, scoring three runs on only one safety. Lonnie was brought on in relief and threw 2 2/3 innings of hitless ball. Starting pitcher Steve Murdaugh almost worked out of a bases-loaded, no-out jam in the bottom of the eighth but walked Jim Logan on four pitches, forcing in the winning run as we took a 4-3 victory. After seven straight league titles CMI had been topped by Horton's in a convincing manner. CMI would return to the regional tournament as defending champion. We still had to get through the always tough Springfield district.

At some point during the year Lonnie had gotten stuck with the nickname of Lon Juan for no apparent reason. At the Jefferson City tournament we had a large group gathered in a motel room between games and were watching an old TV cartoon starring two little boys called Spud and Wheezer. Someone thought they closely resembled Rod Towe and Randy Johnson so they were instantly gifted with those nicknames. Jim Logan had amused himself one game when Randy was poised to catch a game ending popup yelling, "Squeeze 'er, Wheezer!" Jerry Mallonee seemed to like the ring of the name Jack Cannon, Jefferson City's catcher, so he titled Rod Towe with the name "Fat Jack Cannon" because of his hitting prowess, "Fat Jack" for short. Younger brother Randy was called "Toy".

The district started with a big upset as Northern Lights defeated favored Marshfield 3-0 behind John Carr's three hitter. We topped open league club Love Oil 7-2 with Rod Towe lining a homerun off hurler Larry Marshall. Next, Lonnie was superb beating Foremost and pitcher Earl Rivers 2-0 guaranteeing us a berth in the state tournament in Jeff City. Stewart won against Har-Bell 9-2 in the winner's finals. In the loser's finals Mallonee and Har-Bell defeated Marshfield 6-2. Lonnie was sailing along in the first game of the finals 1-0 against Har-Bell and Mallonee when they pushed across two runs in the bottom of the ninth to force another game. Gus Henry's grand slam in the final game was the big blow as we won 7-2. Our confidence was high as we headed to the state tournament.

We had won the league championship, the city tournament and the district, which gave us a good draw in the state bracket. We had added Wayne Ryan from Foremost for some extra pop in the lineup. Steve Stewart started things off with a two hitter, beating Harold's of Lexington 8-0 in five innings. I followed with a one hitter, getting by New Haven 5-1. Lonnie out dueled Hannibal's "Rocket" Givens for a 4-1 win. Next up was the powerful St. Joseph Walnut Products team with "Doc" Miller on the mound. After 13 grueling innings and a major collision at the plate between solidly built Randy Johnson and catcher Leo Blakely, who managed to hold onto the ball, in the bottom of the seventh Lonnie came out the winner. With the score 0-0, Jim Logan got on first base and quickly stole second. Wayne Ryan came through again with a single, driving in Logan with the winning run.

Walnut Woods, also from St. Joe, was the opponent in the winner's bracket finals, with Herb "Ironman" Lucas doing the pitching. There had been lots of rain during the tournament and the fields were a mess. Duensing was the only diamond left in somewhat playable condition. The loser's bracket games were being played at Eagles field, with the plate and infield reversed so hitters were batting at the centerfield fence with the wet slick grass as the infield. The outfielders had to manage the mud of the former dirt infield. As we arrived at the park, we were confronted with two problems. The grounds crew at Duensing had mired a dump truck in the outfield behind second base and couldn't get it out. Fred Harrison had driven his car up to the tournament and somehow had locked all our bats and balls in the trunk of his car. After taking a great amount of abuse from most of the team Fred managed to open up enough room behind the back seat to allow his younger brother Donnie to squeeze through and pop the trunk. Fred was saved! Ryan had walked to the truck deep in mud and offered to drive it out. The grounds crew didn't think it was possible but he drove it out quite easily.

With "Lon Juan" again on the rubber we disposed of Woods 5-2 and for the second year in a row we were in the state finals, but this time we were in the driver's seat. Walnut had won the loser's finals, and we would play them for the title. With all the rain and mud, playing the finals later in the week was discussed. State commissioner Fred Hoffman wanted to move the games to St. Joseph's Walnut Park. Jim Horton refused, thinking the games should be in Springfield since we were the only undefeated team. It was finally decided to finish the tournament in the muck of Duensing field. It would be Lonnie throwing for us again and Miller on the mound for Walnut. It was 1-1 going into the sixth when Walnut third baseman Jerry McDaniel singled to right putting them ahead 2-1. Gus Henry tripled in the bottom of the inning with one out, but Miller got a strikeout and a pop up to get out of the jam. We faltered in the last game, getting shutout by tall left-hander Tim Reynolds 6-0. We had started Lonnie again but he ran into trouble early and Stewart relieved in the second inning.

But the damage had been done as we again took second-place. This time, however, there was a silver lining. Due to ASA rule changes, Walnut would automatically represent Missouri in the national tournament and we would get a trip to the regionals in Lincoln, Nebraska, joining defending champion CMI in the championship.

We hurriedly made preparations for the trip to Lincoln. Duke and Anita Henry inquired about renting a bus for the trip. The bus company had only one bus available for the weekend and they were told another team had asked about it. Knowing that the other team was CMI, Duke quickly reserved it without knowing how we would raise the money. The team gathered enough sponsors to pay for the bus and we headed to the regionals in style.

The rain followed us to Nebraska and the four-day tournament was condensed to two days, which means teams were playing all night Sunday. CMI was upset in the opener, losing 3-1 to host team Lincoln, getting only two hits off their pitcher as Steve Murdaugh took the loss. Horton's led off the tournament with Lonnie topping Topeka, Kansas, and followed with pick-up pitcher Phil Wilkinson dominating St. Louis Kutis 2-0. Wilkinson held the great hitting St. Louis team to two hits and never allowed a ball to be pulled, with everything going to the opposite field. In the winner's bracket finals Lonnie held Modern Piping from Cedar Rapids, Iowa, to four hits. Wilkinson relieved in the top of the $12^{th}$ to keep the game scoreless going into the bottom of the inning. Noting that he had "never seen a left hander he couldn't hit", Steve Hutton came off the bench to pinch hit. Facing him on the mound was lefty Bobby Moore, one of the best southpaws in the game. True to his word, "Hut" lined a single to right field to start the inning. Jim Logan was called on to pinch run and stole second. Wayne Ryan followed through again with a base hit through the middle, scoring Logan to put us into the finals.

While we slept, CMI won five games in the loser's division playing all though the day and night. Beau Robinson remembered standing in center field and watching the sun come up knowing that they had several more games to play if they kept winning. We squared off against CMI in the finals knowing they would have to beat us twice for the title. It would be CMI's Roy Burlison on the hill to battle Phil Wilkinson pitching for Horton's. We jumped to a

3-1 lead going into the sixth when CMI rallied to tie it up 3-3. Lonnie came into the game to settle things down. Mike Brooks opened the top of the seventh with a ground ball, pinch hit single off Burlison's leg. Gus Henry doubled down the right field line, putting runners on second and third with one out. Wayne Ryan flied to center field with Brooks tagging up and scoring as Robinson's throw to the plate hit the second base umpire. Randy Johnson singled in another run before CMI relieved with Murdaugh who was met with an inside the park home run over the left fielder's head by Mark Gann giving Horton's an 8-3 lead and the win. Lonnie shared the Most Valuable Player award with Burlison. At the age of 18 Lonnie had become a dominant pitcher with good "stuff", a cool head and the confidence of a much older hurler. On to Midland, Michigan, for the national tournament!

Our Horton's team's great play faltered at the nationals. We drew Flint, Michigan, in the opener. Between several debatable illegal pitch calls against Lonnie and Phil, who relieved in the fifth, and three errors we were on the losing end of a 7-3 decision. Horton's came back, with Wilkinson throwing against Buchanan, New York, and posting a 4-0, three hit shutout. Mark Gann doubled in the third inning and eventually scored on Wilkinson's sacrifice fly. We wrapped it up with three runs in the fourth, with Randy Johnson's double and Jim Logan's squeeze bunt being the key hits. The renowned Clearwater, Florida, bombers was the next test, and we were defeated 5-1 with Jim March driving in our only run. We finished a disappointing 1-2 and a 14$^{th}$ place finish. On a good note, we would have an automatic regional spot next year to defend our title.

# TWENTY-THREE

## SHORT STAY ON TOP

Our elation over our regional win and the disappointment of our showing at the national tournament was soon overshadowed by another blow to our continued success. Our hated rival, CMI, had sweet talked Lonnie into joining their team. Lonnie, at age 18, had tied the record for youngest pitcher to ever win a regional, matching the feat performed by his father, in 1957. Now, for the second year in a row, Jim Little again had stolen our ace. It was not because he could help them, he still had Roy Burlison on staff, but because Lonnie could hurt them if he pitched for us. We had a long winter to mull this over and devise a new strategy for the coming year.

Springfield had received the bid to host the national tournament in 1978 and once again the AAA league winner would serve as host. CMI had already bolstered their roster by adding great hitters Al and Ted Hicks from St. Joseph's Roto-Rooter team, as well as ace St. Joe Walnut Product pitcher Tim Reynolds. Even though we were guaranteed a spot at the regional meet in Cedar Rapids, Iowa, as defending champions it would be a lot cheaper and an easier course to the nationals serving as host team rather than having to win the regional. Mike Larmer came through with a sponsor from the company he worked for, Ken's Pizza, so we at least didn't have to scramble for funds for the coming year. It was decided that there wasn't another pitcher available to help us a great deal so we could always pick one up after the state or regional. That left the job of winning the league up to our hitting and a step up by pitchers Steve Stewart and me. We went into league play with all of us feeling a lot of pressure to either repeat our league win or again win a tough regional.

   This was the first time we had the services of Steve Stewart for the whole year and he quickly showed the promise of his years to come. Stewart was tough and started the year with several winning outings while I faltered out of the gate. An exceptionally rainy spring kept us from becoming consistent. Burlison shut us out in our first meeting, winning a 4-0 decision. We dropped games to Har-Bell and Foremost early on and the rest of the year was an uphill climb. Besides CMI bolstering their lineup, The Players, the former Frost's team, added pitcher Kenny Williams and Tommy Smith and would field a really good team. The Foremost squad had tacked on perennial top hitter Jim Maggi and power hitting Louie Bunch to go with pitchers Tim Buff and Earl Rivers. Har-Bell stocked up on power with the addition of Stu Dunlop and Charlie Essary. Gary Augustine and Jerry Mallonee would again be the hurlers. Northern Lights had pitchers John Carr who was showing great promise and Steve Hansen. They were solid with the likes of Alan Potts, John Maritt, Dave McBeath and Rondell Miller at the plate.

   Brother Jim and I spent a lot of nights at Doling Park watching some open league contests and became good friends with John Carr, who also lived in the neighborhood and shared our love of the game. One night after AAA league games we joined Carr and some of the Northern Lights squad at a downtown bar. Outfielder Robby Arbaugh was relating how he had happened to drive by a grade school where teacher "Big Al" Potts was providing physical education to a bunch of elementary kids. Arbaugh said Al, at 6'6" and 280 pounds, looked like Gulliver meeting the Lilliputians. One of my favorite memories of Doling Park was a league makeup game between CMI and the old 89'er Restaurant team. Larry Hale was going from first to third on a base hit when the throw got away from the third baseman and rolled down the fence toward the outfield. Hale jumped to his feet and darted down the baseline for home. 89'er coach Chuck Middleton was smoking a cigarette on the sideline and calmly picked up the ball and threw a strike to the catcher with the umpire calling Hale out. None of the umps had noticed that Chuck had picked the ball up and didn't change the call. CMI protested a great length but to no avail. On another evening I was watching brother Jim and good friend Steve Hutsell play an open league game. Their catcher Mike Coveyough loved to play but didn't possess a lot of talent. With a runner headed to the plate Jim took a cut off throw from the outfield and delivered a perfect toss to the plate. Mike was wearing shin guards and the ball went untouched between his hands and caromed off his knee back into the outfield. Hutsell couldn't stop laughing from his shortstop position.

Our Ken's Pizza team performed better later in the year, with an improved league second half record including a 5-4 win over CMI and Lonnie Marshall, but finished a disappointing third-place. We had played well at the highly regarded Nashville, Tennessee, tournament taking a shutout victory over former national tournament entry Atlanta, Georgia, after they had topped CMI and Roy Burleson in the previous game. We lost to Tulsa, Oklahoma, with Stewart throwing a good winner's final game before we were eliminated by CMI 3-0 in the loser's bracket. We did have outstanding performances over the year from Mike Brooks, Rod Towe and Randy Johnson, with all three finishing in the league's top ten hitters. CMI easily won the league and would host the nationals in Springfield. They also had had three top ten finishers headed by Bonus Frost, with Beau Robinson and Clem Quillman joining in. The top average, however, went to Har-Bell's Stu Dunlop. Beau's hefty total of seven home runs was topped only by teammate Ted Hicks' nine.

1978 Ken's Pizza

Front row: Rod Towe, Steve Stewart

Second row-Mike Brooks, Steve Hutton, Joe Henry, Mike McTeer

Third row-Mark Gann, Randy Johnson, Roger Cromer, Jim Logan

Fourth row-Jim Horton, Gus Henry, Jim March, Danny Miles, Mike Egly

    We journeyed to Cedar Rapids, Iowa, to defend our regional title with the additions of hurler Steve Murdaugh and outfielder Mike Egly from the Players team. I pitched the opener against Iowa State winner Cedar Rapids Butt'R Top, suffering a 4-0 loss to pitcher Dale Root. After the game we discovered that beer was sold at the ballpark and we drowned our sorrows down the third base line bleachers. We loosened up after a few beers and all the pressure we had put on ourselves over the summer was released. We all had pushed too hard to overcome the loss of Lonnie on the mound and I think that accounted for a lot of our poor showing during the year. We apparently entertained a least part of the crowd with our challenge races and laughter. One observer noted, "They should have shown that much enthusiasm during the game." There was a snow fence around the park and on the way back to the cars we just climbed over it. Except for Stewart who calmly placed his ditty bag over the fence, stepped back a couple of steps and attempted to jump the short barrier. His foot slipped and he slid through the grass beneath the fence, picked up his bag, and proceeded to the cars. Steve came back to throw a four hitter against Broken Bow, Nebraska, in our 5-0 win.

Next up was our old enemy Topeka, Kansas, and thrower Charley Rappard. Steve Murdaugh drew the assignment and we jumped out to a 6-1 lead. The Kansas team came back to tie in the fourth, chasing Murt. I threw okay for a couple of innings and we went into the seventh ahead 10-8. They scored five runs in the inning after a debatable call at second which got manager Jim Horton ejected for arguing. With two outs and the bases loaded and Joe Henry at the plate, Stewart turned to Horton in the stands and asked if he wanted a pinch runner for Roger Cromer on first base. The third-place umpire overheard the conversation and called a forfeit. We naturally exploded with the abrupt end of our tournament and we followed the umps into the parking lot. Mike McTeer picked up a rock to hurl their way but his arm was blocked by Randy Johnson. It was perhaps" Wheezer's" best defensive play of the year.

The National Tournament was a great showing by CMI and the city of Springfield. Behind Burleson, the CMI team made it to the winner's finals before losing 1-0 to Reading, Pennsylvania, and left-handed pitcher Ty Stofflet. The next day they drew Clearwater, Florida, and ace Joe Lynch. It was another 1-0 game with Lynch skying a home run over the left center field fence for the only run. With CMI in the running for the whole tournament the crowds swelled with over 80,000 fans entering the park over nine days. At the time it was a national tournament record for attendance. Springfield loved softball.

# TWENTY-FOUR

## RESHUFFLE

Everything changes for the better or the worse depending upon your perspective. CMI's great run at the nationals had led to several of their players being inviting to tryouts for a United States team to play in the Pan American games during the summer. Ted Hicks had established new national tournament records for hits with 12 and average at .632. Larry Hale, Bonus Frost and Jim Nickels received invitations, but Ted was the only one selected to make the team. Ted had agreed to play for a team in Midland, Michigan, and would be joined there by Lonnie Marshall and Joe Henry. Manager Jim Little had lost sponsor CMI and decided to combine the remainder of his team with Jim Veith's Jefferson City team to be called the Gaslight Chiefs. They would be without the services of Roy Burlison for most of the year and would play league games in Jeff City with pitchers Tim Reynolds and Gary McDaniel, leaving the Springfield AAA league open for the crowning of a new champion. The league expanded quickly into a seven-team league for the first time in several years.

Marshfield Mill, sponsored by Gayford and Jerry Crawford, had assembled a really good team anchored by pitchers Steve Murdaugh and Jim Collins. Manager and third baseman Jim Rader featured an outfield of Mike Egly, Kenny Brown and Harold Harris. The infield would be Mike Brooks at first, Jim March at second, and Tommy Smith at short, with Ronnie Crosswhite and Rod Jones splitting catching duties. Builders Glass would be a contender with Tim Buff on the mound joined by Russ Strunk and Earl Rivers. They had a formidable hitting contingency of Wayne Ryan, Steve Hutchinson, Jim McDaniel, Louie Bunch, Jim Maggi, Bonus Frost, Don Henderson, Bill Helfrect and Donnie Haworth. Ancil Fry would again play third base and, with the withdrawal of Foremost as a sponsor, it would be the first time in 22 years he would not be wearing their uniform.

Sammy Potter had put together a new team anchored by Denver Dixon and included several of the old Har-Bell team, Gary Palmer, Jim Dopp, Ben Upp, Larry Cotter and Steve Stombaugh. Monte Clithero had played on the two-time state winner Jefferson City Mousy's and would man center field. Up and coming hurler John Carr would be joined by left-hander Bob Crowell. Al Hansen would be managing Bus's Casuals and had secured the services of veteran pitcher Ken Williams, Jim Evans, and young throwers Tim Baker and Steve Hansen. Bus's lineup would include Alan Potts, Jerry Agee, Dave McBeath, Mark Randolph, Bob Gleghorn, Tommy Freeman and David Melton. The catcher would be Craig Alexander.

Also joining the mix would be two young teams, the Bottlers and Pratt-Lambert. The Bottlers had pitchers Gary Augustine, Ron Gove and Gary Taylor. Outfielders included Jim Logan, Randy Crocker, David Frost, Mike Manes and Ron Barber. The infield would consist of Mark Harrell at first, Donnie Johnson at second, Stan Jinx at short, Kent Leeper catching, and Gary Stracke at third. Pratt–Lambert had some great young talent. Center fielder Rick Young was a gifted and exciting player, as was shortstop David Rothermel. They would be joined by infielders Wes Towe, Bruce Johnson and David Chambers. Other outfielders were Randy Nichols, Curt Rogers and Greg McTeer. Catcher Rondell Miller would handle pitchers Jerry Wampler, Ray Fuerst and Dave Boyer.

With manager Jim Horton enduring an unfair and unmerited year-long suspension from the Springfield Park Board, Rod Towe stepped into the managerial role and added Har-Bell as a sponsor and revamped our team. Slick fielding second baseman Randy

Towe was added along with power hitter Stu Dunlop, fleet outfielders Larry Plaster and John Maritt, and pitcher Jerry Mallonee. With the adoption of the new designated hitter rule we could add hitter Charlie Essary. The team retained Steve Hutton, Gus Henry, Mark Gann, Randy Johnson, Mike McTeer, and pitchers Steve Stewart and me. Over a four-year period, we had lost five members of the original Horton's team that had been so successful. We had earned a trip to the national tournament, played in two regionals winning one, finished with two runners up and a fourth place in state play and had broken CMI's seven-year run as league champions, securing a spot as one of the top teams in the Midwest. That would soon be all in the past as we set a new course with a rebuilt team.

The interest in fast pitch was showing a decline overall with fewer open league and church league teams in Springfield. In St Joseph they had to form a travel league to get consistent competition for twice defending state champion Walnut Products. Teams from St Joe had won the last three state tournaments and Walnut would be the team to beat in '79. They would be faced with winning over two or three good Springfield teams in addition to the Gaslight team that would have to now qualify for regional and national trips through the state meet.

Our Har-Bell team started out the league with early losses to Builders Glass, The Bottlers, Pratt-Lambert and Marshfield before righting the ship. Playing under the Ken's Pizza banner last year we had taken third in the Nashville, Tennessee, tournament, losing to CMI and the Tulsa Firebirds, and we entered that tournament for a second time. We had to scramble for players to make the trip and we added pitcher John Carr, second baseman Wes Towe, and surprisingly Steve Stombaugh who just happened to drive down with John Maritt to watch the tournament. We topped Nashville 2-1 in 12 innings in the first game, pounded a team from Ruby Falls, Tennessee, before losing 7-6 to Tuscaloosa, Alabama. We rebounded with wins over Grand Rapids, Michigan, 9-1 and Charleston, South Carolina, 6-3. The next day we won the prestigious tournament by defeating Greenville, South Carolina, 5-0 and 3-1. John Carr pitched a one hitter in the first game with Wes Towe slamming a three-run homer. Jerry Mallonee hurled the championship game and Larry Plaster added a home run. We also won a good tournament in Jefferson City as we topped Harold's of Lexington 6-2 in the title game. Steve Stewart was named Most Valuable Pitcher winning two games and relieving in two more wins.

The second half of the league saw us play much better but we finished one game behind Marshfield in the standings. We had defeated them three times in the league, but they had only lost two other games to earn the championship. Jim Little had gotten a new sponsor, O'Byrne Electric, for the end of the year and had regained the services of Roy Burlison for state play. Marshfield's business manager had somehow forgotten to enter the team in the district and had to gain a judge's verdict to allow them to participate. Sammy Potter and Denver Dixon had jumped to O'Byrne from Sun Twin, leaving that team in dire straits to qualify for the state. We played O'Byrne in the winner's bracket semifinals, which would have earned us a state berth but second baseman Gary Bremmerkamp's liner to left field in the second inning drove in the winning run. We lost as Tim Reynolds shut us out 1-0. We came up one run short again losing to Bus's 3-2 and, for the first time in seven years, my team would not be going to the state.

1980 O'Byrne Electric

Front row: Larry Robinson, Jim Little, Sam Potter, Steve Stombaugh, Don Johnson, Monte Clithero

Back Row: Beau Robinson, Ed Johnson, Ken Noble, Tom Smith, Bill Marler, Wayne Ryan, Jerry Bernet, Junior Williams, Roy Burlison, Jim Nichols, John Younger, Larry Hale

Veteran throwers Tim Buff of Builder's Glass and Jim Collins of Marshfield had led the league in wins with records of 10-2. Steve Murdaugh had a record of 9-3 while Jerry Mallonee and John Carr both had won eight games. At the state tournament pitcher Jim Collins had no hit champion Walnut Products for three innings and he told Marshfield manager Jim Rader they always got to him the second time through the order. Sure enough, the next inning the St. Joe team smashed three consecutive home runs. When manager Rader walked to the mound to make a pitching change, he said, "You know, Jim, I was thinking about leaving you in just to see how many homeruns they could hit!" O'Byrne would be returning to the national tournament by taking down powerful St. Joe Walnut 3-2 in the state finals with Burleson saving the victory for starting pitcher Tim Reynolds.

## TWENTY-FIVE

### WONDER WOMEN

Womens fastpitch in Springfield began in the mid 1930's when games were played on fields at Drury College, Phelps Grove Park and Grant Beach Park. The first lights to be added by the park board were installed at Grant Beach in 1934. Two early pitchers of note were Dorothy Robinson and Greta Lee Reese throwing for the Toombs-Fay team as she fashioned seven no-hitters for the year. Springfield began coming to the forefront in 1950 with the Y-Ettes taking second-place in the state tournament behind the pitching of Ann King. The solid Central Labor Union squad took titles in 1951, 1952, 1955, and 1956 with Oletha Mosby doing the early pitching with Ann King and Jorita Rossen becoming the mainstays later on. The team added second-place finishes in 1953 and 1954. Other corps members included Evelyn Gates, Violet Conard, Wanda Edmonson, Pat Cantrell, Joan Pearl, Barbara Shockley, Jeanne Burgess, Helen Gorman, Joan Owens, Millie Ayers, Sandra Bowen, Sarah Horn, and Iola Meece. The decade ended with teams sponsored by Barnes Store winning the state meet in 1957, 1958, and 1959 before being upset by Springfield's Knockers in the 1960 tournament.

The 1960s started out with St. Joseph clubs taking state laurels in 1961 and 1962 before Royal Crown broke through in 1963 with a run to the title. Sherry Evans did mound duty for the second-place 1964 Barnes Store team. Barnes Store finished its sponsorship in 1965 after grabbing a state tournament title with the help of the pitching from Ann King and the timely hitting of Shirley Simmons, Artie Hubbard, Donna Bilyeu, and Barbara Peltz. The Bethany CTs went on a tear winning five of the next six tournaments due to the pitching heroics of Peggy Kirkland and Charlotte Stamper with only the Neosho Gidgets breaking the string with Shirley Rosiere on the hill in 1968. One of the stars of the league was pitcher and good hitter Kay Hunter. She was a teacher at then Southwest Missouri State College and would become the coach of the school's women's softball team from its origination in the early '70s until the early '80s. With women athletes from the SMS Physical Education department, she built a strong club sponsored by Foremost Dairy. The team took second-place in state play in 1969 with Hunter being joined on the mound by SMS coach Reba Sims along with hitters Brenda Senseney, Sue Schuble, Linda Dollar, Jan Trotter, and Laura Goddard. The 1970 team hosted the regional meet in Springfield with Billie Jo Goodman, Jan Crumply, and Jackie Tekotte having impressive performances. The Foremost team finally garnered a state championship in 1972 topping the CTs as Hunter recorded four wins and Cindy Henderson tossed the winning final. Dr. Mary Jo Wynn had established SMS's women's sports teams in the late '50s with tennis and volleyball squads and was ahead of her time as a harbinger of the federally mandated Title IX that began the movement to gain equality in college sports programs. The early SMS softball teams beginning in the '70s were among the best in the country and those teams stayed together to play in the city's summer leagues. With power pitcher Cindy Henderson on the mound the SMS team won an AIWA national title in '74 and finished in the top four two more years.

Those pioneer athletes included Sue Schuble, Linda Dollar, Jackie Tekotte and Carol Myers. Sue Schuble played on and coached several state and regional tournament winners and national tournament contenders. Sue also became a legendary basketball coach at Kickapoo High School in Springfield, winning state titles at the highest level. Linda Dollar joined Schuble on those softball teams, and the volleyball teams she later coached at SMS won more than 750 games and earned many trips to the NCAA national tournament. Cindy Henderson and Carol Myers played professionally on women's softball teams in Detroit, Michigan, and St. Louis. Henderson was one of the most successful pitchers in that league. Most of those early athletes played multiple sports, including volleyball, basketball and field hockey with Reba Sims coaching and, because of underfunding, used the same uniforms for every sport. These talented women and others established the framework for future Missouri State University Lady Bears softball, volleyball and basketball team successes and helped promote women's athletics nationwide.

The two power houses in Missouri women's softball at the time were Springfield Foremost, with basically the SMS softball team, and the North Missouri CT's. Foremost had topped defending champ CT's in 1974 and the two looked like the likely contenders in 1975. Sue Schuble had married Steve Murdaugh and was playing for Foremost and coaching a young team of high school women she had assembled called Big Blue. With the talented Penny Clayton on the mound Big Blue had surprised everyone and topped the CT's for the state title. The team featured sisters Mary and Joannie French, Jean Eubanks, Regi Martin, Elaine Fields, Cathy Bishop, and the great swing of third baseman Lisa Nicholson. Those players would be the nucleus of the SMS team and Frost's Sporting Goods team for the next four years. Another pitcher of note in those two years was Springfieldian Kay Caldwell. Kay had been tutored by Steve Murdaugh and toiled on the mound for Nevada, Missouri, at state play. Penny Clayton's father, Richard, worked with my dad and had asked me to coach her when she was in high school. I explained how to throw a rise ball and after a few tosses to catcher Regi Martin she completely had it down. Definitely a quick learner. Regi's older brother Danny happened to be Lonnie Marshall's catcher in their young men's days. The North Missouri CT's came back to top the Frost's women (formerly Big Blue) in the '76 state tournament only to see Frost regain the title in '77 and finish seventh at the national tournament in Hayward, California. Earlier that year the SMS team finished second in the college regional finals losing to eventual national champion Northern Iowa University.

The SMS squad advanced to the college national tournament in 1978 behind the pitching of Penny Clayton and Tammi Long. Chris Dufner and Jackie Tekotte were invited to try out for the United States Pan American team while pitcher Cindy Henderson and Carol Myers continued playing with St. Louis and Buffalo, New York, respectfully. The best hitter, however, was Lisa Nicholson. The left-handed batter was a good third baseman with an excellent arm but really excelled at the plate. She had a smooth, sweeping swing that was a picture of perfection. Softballs literally jumped off her bat on contact as she nailed liner after liner through the defense. After graduation she devoted her life to missionary work.

Springfield had received the bid to hold the ASA Women's National Tournament in 1979 and the Frost's team earned the right to serve as host team. Unfortunately, their ace, Penny Clayton, had developed a severe case of tendonitis and was restricted in her mound appearances. Penny was also solid at the plate and started several games as the designated hitter. The team finished a solid seventh place to continue to be one of the top 10 teams at the college and ASA national levels. Lisa Nicholson was selected to the ASA all-tournament team. Crowds of 2,500 to 3,000 fans crowded the stands at Thompson Field each night of the tournament to watch the top-level women's teams compete.

The following season saw Clayton struggling with her injury throughout the SMS college season. Her doctor had equipped her with four electrodes wired from her shoulder to a battery strapped to her waist. It was designed for use after pitching to relieve the pain. Behind the pitching of Tammi Long and Sherry Rouner and the ball bashing of Diane Cline the team had advanced to the championship game of the college regional against Creighton University. It was decided to let Clayton try to pitch with the electrodes attached during a game. The procedure worked, stopping the pain during the game as she shut out the Creighton squad, winning 1-0 in twelve innings sending the club to another national tournament. Penny Clayton proved to be the fast pitch bionic woman. Ironically, one of the SMS losses in the tournament was to 1-0 to Texas A&M, with Clayton losing to pitcher Lori Stoll who pitched in the summer for the North Missouri CT's.

Springfield had long held a women's tournament, but in 1980 there was not a single fast pitch team to serve as host. The Frost's team had broken up, with several of the college team going to play in St. Louis. Kay Hunter was asked to put together a team to compete in the tournament. They played competitively and went on to only play exhibition games throughout the year. Amazingly, the team rallied to finish second in the state tournament. Softball would continue to be a successful sport for the university but the summer leagues would never recover. The "wonder women" of Springfield's national tournament competitors performed in the decade of the '70s and left a great tradition of determination and talent for young women for years to come.

## TWENTY-SIX

### THE BRIGHT LIGHTS GET DIMMER

Springfield fast pitch softball had held its own during the '70s with strong teams and a consistent fan base. Teams from the city had a streak of six straight state champions, beginning with Foremost in 1967 and ending with Scenic Shopper in 1972, and then winding up with O'Bryne Electric's title over St. Joseph's Walnut Products team in 1979. As dominant as manager Ed Bremer's teams had been in the '50s and Larry Atwood's clubs in the '60s, Jim Little's teams of the '70s had been by far the most successful. In the decade of the '70s Little's teams had won the AAA league title nine times, won all three state tournaments they entered, played in eight regionals and winning seven times, earned the national host team spot twice, and played in nine national tournaments with two third-place finishes. They were easily one of the top five teams in the country during that time. O'Bryne took sixth place at the '79 national tournament, losing in nine innings to host team Midland, Michigan, 1-0 with Midland scoring on a squeeze play and giving the victory to imported New Zealand thrower Owen "Fog" Walford. Santa Rosa then topped them 7-0 in the loser's bracket.

It was also the end of an era for softball beat writer Dave

Schulty who had covered Springfield softball for well over a decade. The Springfield Newspaper had been sold to the Gannett Corporation and lots of changes were taking place within the organization which would deeply impact coverage of local sports.

Our Har-Bell team would stay pretty much intact for the 1980 season except for the departure of designated hitter Charley Essary, who had set a record with his lofty .534 batting average in leading the league, and the addition of new manager Denny Henry. The Har-Bell team continued to be a force on the road, finishing second at the West Plains and St. Joseph tournaments and winning at Jefferson City. Steve Stewart came into his own by beating O'Bryne twice in the league. Another team victory over them meant that we had handed them three of their four league losses. Our team was solid, with outfielders Stu Dunlop, John Maritt, and Larry Plaster in the outfield, catcher Mark Gann, and an infield of Rod Towe, Steve Hutton, Randy Towe, Jim Rader and Gus Henry. Mike Egly joined the team halfway through the season and swung a big bat along with designated hitter Ron Crosswhite.

The season was also marked by the passing of pitcher Gary Augustine who was undergoing a kidney transplant at the age of 29. Gary worked for the local Dr. Pepper bottler and was the son of the Bottler's manager and concessioner Leo Augustine. He was the third pitcher to lose his life too early during my career. We had earlier lost hurlers Gene Barr and Eddie Brooks. Eddie had lost his life serving in the Viet Nam War.

Springfield would entertain the Young Men's National Tournament in '80 featuring host team Coley's Restaurant and the defending champion Schlitz Bulls. The Bulls had won two 14-16-year-old national tournaments and a 17-18-year-old championship in '79 under the sponsorship of Empire Bank. Coley's was managed by Gene Brown and the team featured several players from his family, in particular power hitter and pitcher Berrah Brown. The Bulls would ride the strong right arm of pitcher Doug Middleton and the hitting of Rick Ellsworth, Scott Loveland, Barry Marshall and Chris Lane to earn its fourth straight national title. As in the previous year the Bulls came back through the loser's bracket to win twice in the finals.

Steve Hutton had put on a show in the St. Joseph tournament leading Har-Bell to four wins on Saturday. After pulling a thigh muscle in the first game he smacked a three-run homer against Des Moines Reames Food to give pitcher Jerry Mallonee a 3-1 win. Serving as the designated hitter, Hutton drove in the winning run in the bottom of the seventh as Steve Stewart got the 2-1 victory over the Tulsa Firebirds. We then bounced Iowa-Walnut as Steve totaled seven hits in three games. Mallonee defeated the Des Moines Bombers 2-1 before Clearlake, Iowa, scored all seven of their runs in the sixth inning to eliminate our team 7-2.

For the first time the district tournament would be held at Thompson field, which had been used as the national tournament field for the last three Springfield hosted tournaments. In an early game we had runners at first and third when we got a fly ball fairly deep into left field. Jim Rader was the runner at first and, being fundamentally sound, went halfway between first and second as the ball took flight. The runner on third tagged up after the catch and raced home to score, drawing a throw from the outfield. Noticing that none of the umpires were watching him Rader simply trotted to second without going back to the base to tag. The team appealed the play but the umpires couldn't change the call because they had not seen the play. When Rader came back to the bench at the end of the inning I asked, "Jim, aren't you supposed to tag up on a fly out?" Rader replied, "If I had done that, I would never have made it to second." Unfortunately, that game was the highlight of our tournament. Bus's pitcher Jim Evans had defeated us last year in the district keeping us out of the state and proved to be an even bigger nemesis as he beat us twice, 5-1 and 6-5, eliminating us once again.

O'Bryne Electric had won the district behind the pitching of transplants Bill Marler and Edmore Johnson. Marler was from St. Louis and had a good drop ball and a lot of speed. Johnson was from Detroit and had thrown amazingly well at the national tournament level and at the time was one of the top left-handers in the country. We had faced him several years earlier when playing for Crowe's Restaurants, and he had only gotten better. The Springfield Merchants took second in the district and picked up Rod Towe and myself to join them at the state tournament in Jefferson City. Behind the good pitching of Tim Buff and Steve Murdaugh they managed a third-place finish to qualify for the regional. Walnut Products had emerged from the loser's bracket to beat the heavily favored O'Bryne team 5-0 in 14 innings and 4-0 in the championship game due to the great pitching of Tim Reynolds and Herb Lucas.

O'Bryne would join the Merchants in the regional meet in Kansas City. The Merchants had a solid squad with an infield of Ancil Fry, Jeff Richards, Jim March and Mike Brooks, outfielders Jim Maggi, Bill Helfrecht, Larry Cotter and Kenny Brown, and catchers Donnie Haworth and Ron Hubbard. They won one game and lost two in a disappointing finish. O'Bryne lost 2-1 to Cedar Rapids, Iowa, with Jerry Rauch on the mound and Roy Burlison taking the loss. St. Louis Kutis plated two runners in the seventh inning for a come from behind decision taking the O' Bryne team out of the tournament. The good hitting of Wayne Ryan, Tom Smith, Beau Robinson, Larry Hale, Bonus Frost and others had been silenced late in the state meet and that trend had continued into the regional. There would be no national tournament appearance for them in 1980. The '80s were going to be different for a lot of teams.

# TWENTY-SEVEN

## *Gut Check*

After a disappointing 1980 Jim Little decided to retool the O'Bryne team and combined part of our Har-Bell team and a few of his holdovers. The key member of the newcomers was Rod Towe who pulled brothers Randy and Wesley and brother-in-law Larry Plaster, along with power hitter Stu Dunlop and the Henry brothers, Gus and Joe, to join the team. Last year players Wayne Ryan, Bonus Frost, Larry Hale, and catcher Jim Nichols were retained to form a strong foundation. Roy Burlison was gone but pitchers Edmore Johnson and Billy Marler would be joined by Lonnie Marshall and new-to-town thrower Charlie Slavens. The changes at the top of the league meant a major reshuffling of the other squads trying to compete.

I had always wanted to manage a team and had become disenchanted with pitching. Our team of the last two years had been successful in winning games but had not finished well, getting upset in the districts and missing the state tournament. Sammy Potter had paid me a visit over the winter and asked me to join a new team to be sponsored by Bus's Casuals. I told him I was getting up my own team with the players left from our Har-Bell club and a few additions. I joked with him, "Hell, Sam, I can get us to the state tournament by myself!" At the time I didn't know Springfield would be limited to two state qualifiers.

With the Har-Bell sponsorship in hand I had pitcher Jerry Mallonee, shortstop Steve Hutton, outfielder John Maritt and, most importantly, catcher Mark Gann. I was able to recruit the Rice brothers, Robert and Mark, and Walmart spinoffs Glenn Haworth and the speedy and powerful Rick Young. We added gamer Steve Stombaugh, Richie Gleghorn, Ronnie Crosswhite and Mike Manes. The best "get" for us was constantly improving hurler John Carr. I was confident his pitching would keep getting better under the guidance of Gann behind the plate. We had speed, power, good mechanics and a solid defense except for one valuable asset. We had a large hole at second base and, no matter how we moved guys around, our infield was always weak at one position. That situation haunted us throughout the first half of the season with several games lost by poor defense although the offense was formidable.

Rick Young was considered a bit of "wild card" by most of the league, with great natural talent and questionable attitude. I asked Gann what he thought of Young before we invited him to join and Mark said, "When he is on base you pay attention." I soon discovered Rick actually had a great head, was a good teammate and was highly competitive. He had power, hit for a great average, possessed an outstanding arm and could run like deer. If he had any short-comings it was a lack of fundamentals but with a small amount of coaching, he quickly soaked up all aspects. In order for him to excel I gave him a lot a freedom to use his abundant talents including a green light on the base paths. He also had good instincts and seldom, if ever, made an out while running.

Mark Rice had only played open league ball but had been an outstanding baseball player in high school and college and possessed all the skills necessary to be a great outfielder. John "Packy" Maritt was a solid outfielder with a good arm and speed, and those three together probably formed the best outfield in the league. Glenn "Haystack" Haworth was a solid third sacker with a strong arm and lots of power at the plate. Steve Stombaugh would continue to be the worst practice player I had ever seen and also be one of the most competitive and dependable players come game time. As always, Steve Hutton and Mark Gann were "money" and two of the most underrated players in town. But again, the problem was at second base. Although Gleghorn had been a good third baseman he couldn't adapt, and Mike Manes was a fine offensive player with good speed and a lively bat but defense was foreign to him. As expected, Carr progressed measurably throwing to Gann, but Mallonee suffered from our poor infield and decided to join the Marshfield Mill team for the second half leaving Carr as the only pitcher. Our after-the-game meeting place became Sammy Potter's "Repair Shop Lounge" where our team of mostly bachelors spent a lot of time and a lot of money, but that summer was possibly the most fun I had ever enjoyed. Our core group of Maritt, Stombaugh, Haworth, Carr, Jim and me became close knit and benefited on the field from the camaraderie. We had pretty much been written off as state qualifiers but we knew we had a good team and could compete with anyone in the district. We suffered through a miserable start to the season going 2-9 in the league and not playing much better on the road.

One tournament at Fort Smith, Arkansas, allowed us to pick up O'Bryne hurler Charlie Slavens. Charlie was originally from Springfield and had joined the Marines after graduation. He had just retired as a major in the service after some twenty plus years of duty. He had learned to pitch while deployed and ended up playing in the Washington, D.C., area. He had a good drop ball with plenty of steam on it, but unfortunately was in the same district as Reading, Pennsylvania, and the best left hander on the planet, Ty Stofflet. Charlie kept himself in great condition and had a nasty, competitive attitude on the mound reminding me of Gene Barr. He gained my and all our team's instant respect and came across as you would expect of a military officer. I often joked if they made a movie about Springfield softball he would have to be played by Clint Eastwood. He threw well for us in the tournament, topping a good Tulsa, Oklahoma, team 5-2.

Two things happened in the second half of the year to dynamically change our fortunes. Randy Towe wanted more playing time than he was getting with O'Bryne and joined our club. That instantly made us exceptionally strong up the middle defensively with Gann catching, Hutton and Towe at short and second, and the fleet Rick Young in center. With Mallonee moving to Marshfield John Carr now was throwing twice a week in the league, and nothing makes a pitcher better than lots of work. With those two changes our team jelled and went 9-4 over the last part of the AAA season. We were more than ready for district competition.

O'Bryne had finished the year 22-2 in the league and also played well in an International Softball Congress traveling league finishing just behind winner Fort Worth, Texas, to take third-place and were the odds-on district favorite. Marshfield Mill had taken second in the league behind the pitching of Jim Collins and Jim Evans and the timely hitting of Louie Bunch, Greg Spencer, Richard Ward and Dave Rothermel, but to the good of the rest of the competitors decided to represent their home county. Bus's had had a nice year with a solid defense and a great comeback year for Shelby Hill on the mound winning nine of their 13 games. Jerry Burwell's Magic Country Beef squad was strong with an infield of Ancil Fry, shortstop Jeff Richards, who had been on three young men's national tournament winners, Jim March at second, and first baseman Mike Brooks. The outfield consisted of Harold Harris, Tom Smith, Kenny Brown and Larry Cotter, with Ronnie Hubbard and Donnie Haworth sharing the catching. Brooks, Smith and Brown had fashioned lofty averages, while March, Cotter and Smith had supplied power to the lineup. Tim Buff had injured a shoulder in a tournament and would not pitch the rest of the year. Steve Murdaugh would be joined late in the season by Steve Stewart to give the team a good pitching staff. The Bottler's, with the league's leading hitter Mark Harrell, and Dave Carroll Sports would also join the district meet.

We advanced to the winner's bracket finals in easy fashion and would have to face O'Bryne Electric to qualify for the first state berth granted out of the district. Carr had won a couple of games for us to put us in a good position to have two chances to earn one of the state spots. If we lost to O'Bryne we still had a chance to beat the team coming out of the loser's bracket. I had only thrown a couple of games all year but we decided our chances were better if we saved Carr for the loser's bracket survivor. O'Bryne had endured a long extra inning game with Magic Country Beef the night before and apparently all the stars were in perfect order and the universe was in alignment as fortune smiled upon us. With Slavens on the mound leadoff hitter Rick Young lined the first pitch off the left field foul pole and it hugged the fence line allowing him to round the bases for an inside the park home run. Four innings later he doubled and drove in Mark Gann. That was all the scoring in the game as we won 2-0 catching everyone by surprise. Departing from the park we met the Bus's team coming in to play. As we passed, Sammy Potter asked Carr what time they would be playing us. Carr said, "You are not playing us. You are playing O'Bryne." Their team's jaws dropped. O'Bryne made quick work of Bus's and topped our club twice to win the district, edging Carr 4-3 and winning the last game 7-2. It was on to the state tournament to be played for the first time in Sikeston.

# Twenty-Eight

## A Kiwi for Every Pot

The '81 state tournament was not successful for our Har-Bell team. We lost a heart breaker in our first game losing 3-2 to Cape Girardeau Kelso Supply. The winning run came in the bottom of the sixth and saddled pitcher John Carr with the loss. We won a game behind the pitching of Steve Murdaugh before being shut out by Marshfield Mill hurler Jerry Mallonee 3-0. Murdaugh took the loss against Marshfield with Louie Bunch's two run homer being the biggest blow. The Marshfield team's victory party was cut short by a tragedy as two of their members lost loved ones in a car wreck on their way to Sikeston. Marshfield coach Mike Wolfe lost his wife Bonnie and Jerry Mallonee suffered the loss of his wife, Jane, and eldest son, Jason. Jerry's youngest son Andy was in serious condition at the Poplar Bluff hospital. The Marshfield team had decided not to play, but Mike urged them to continue play in honor of the family lost. It was a tough final two games for the squad but they won 9-3 over Vanduser Budweiser before being eliminated 1-0 in eight innings by Sikeston. Marshfield had won their opener in the tournament by beating Poplar Bluff Budweiser and good thrower Gary Holland 1-0 in nine innings. Upon hearing of the tragedy Holland opened his home to Mallonee for the entire time son Andy was at the Poplar Bluff hospital. It was the first time I realized how tight the fast pitch community was, not just a team or a league, but how it covered the entire state. Jim Little's O'Bryne team came through winning the final game to claim another state title and qualifying for the nationals. The O'Bryne team dedicated the victory to the memory of those who had lost their lives.

O'Bryne quickly picked up Jefferson City Fab's ace hurler Terry Staply who had bested them in the first game of the championship in Sikeston. They made a decent showing at the national tournament losing to defending champion Seattle, Washington, Peterbilt 3-1, defeating Lancaster, California, 5-1, and taking a 2-1 loss in nine innings from Lakewood, California. The Schlitz Bulls young men's team finally tasted defeat losing to Japan in the world tournament and lost to home team Prescott, Arizona, in the national finals. It would mark the last time most of the Bulls would play together, but 6'4" pitcher Doug Middleton was just beginning to make his mark in the softball world.

At some point in time a manager had realized that New Zealand was a hotbed of fast pitch softball. The game had been introduced to the island by United States service men and had exploded in popularity. The interesting part was that seasons were reversed from the United States. While the winter was happening in New Zealand it was summer here. That left a large number of good pitchers available if teams had the financial means to bring them to compete. Several sponsors had that capability with one of the first being Midland, Michigan. They imported "Fog" Wahlburg to pitch for them in the 1979 national tournament. The first real impact was made by Graham Arnold who pitched Seattle, Oregon, Peterbilt to the national title in 1980. At the time top pitchers like Ty Stoffelt, Roy Burlison, Joe Lynch were ending their dominating careers the New Zealand "Kiwis", as we referred to them, were filling in the gaps to keep the game at a highly competitive level. Names like Mike White, Chubb Tangaroa (a native Maori), Pete Meridith, Pete Sandman, Peter Brown, and Steve Schultz soon began popping up with national tournament contenders. The first import into Springfield was young hurler Neal Wardrobe brought in to pitch by manager Al Hanson.

I had reached a point in time where I had a lot of growing up to do and I had parleyed an interest in the restaurant industry into a management job in a bar/restaurant, which severely limited my softball availability. In 1982 manager Ronnie Ghan and business manager Lou Boos had secured a new sponsor in Trailiner Trucking and went to work assembling a league and state contending team. Ghan combined several players from last year's Walmart team with players from our now defunct Har-Bell team. With pitchers Steve Stewart and John Carr and me doing the mound work Mark Gann catching, good hitting and fielding David Rothermel at second, joined with Jeff Richards at shortstop and Rick Young in centerfield, the defense was strong up the middle. Steady players and good hitters Alan Potts at first, Gary Palmer at third, John Maritt and Randy Nichols in the outfield backed by Jerry Agee, Tom Freeman and Mike Manes, all added lots of pop at the plate. The team jelled early and won the first half of the league as Stewart and Carr were awesome on the mound.

The Marshfield team featured Jim Collins and Jim Evans on the mound with the Towe brothers, Rod, Randy and Wes, adding defense and hitting. Power was supplied by Stu Dunlop, Glen Haworth, Rex Holman, Jim Nichols and Larry Plaster, while centerfielder Mark Rice added speed and defense. Bonus Frost sponsored and managed Frost's Sporting Goods with right handers Charley Slavens, Gary McDaniel and Chris Lane on hand. The Henry brothers, Gus and Joe, as well as Barry Marshall, Ben Upp, Larry Hale, David Frost and Marty Little formed the core of the team. Magic Country Beef had Tim Buff, Tim Baker and Doug Middleton hurling with Wayne Ryan, Larry Cotter, Jim Maggi, Ancil Fry and Steve Stombaugh supplying the offense. Steve Murdaugh, Shelby Hill and Jerry Mallonee pitched for Kee Mechanical. Tom Smith, Jim March, Mike Brooks, Louie Bunch, Dave McBeath and Kenny Brown carried the hitting for the squad.

Marshfield edged Frost's for the second half crown. Jim Collins was tough in the league compiling a dominating 13-1 record. Our Trailiner team topped Marshfield in the championship game with Steve Stewart hurling the victory. Alan Potts knocked in the winning run driving in John Maritt. The win garnered Trailiner the host spot in the state with two more teams to qualify through district play. Magic Country and Frost's earned berths, upsetting the good Marshfield team. One of the other state districts did not fill one of their allotted slots so Marshfield was awarded a chance to play in the tournament.

We were playing in the Jefferson City tournament and manager Ronnie Ghan could not be there so I took over as coach for the weekend. One hot, muggy night at Duensing Park John Carr was toiling against the Marshfield team. We were scoring against their pitcher Jim Evans, but they came up with a big inning late in the game. It started with a booted ground ball at second by Jerry Agee who picked it up late and overthrew Potts at first base. The next batter hit a pop up behind second and Agee dropped it. The runner was hung up between second and third. Jerry threw to second but the ball was in the dirt and bounced away from Jeff Richards covering the bag. Jerry quickly picked it up and then threw wildly to third allowing both runs to score. I visited the mound to check on Carr who was fuming. John's glasses were completely fogged over, and I couldn't tell if it was from the humidity or from Agee's antics. Jerry had committed five errors in one inning. The only other error he could have made was a bad throw to the plate but he just didn't get an opportunity to make that one. We finally won the game when Rick Young lined a home run over the left field fence.

The Marshfield team made good use of their gift spot in the state and won the championship over Frost's as more than 9,000 spectators flooded the gates at the Meador Complex. Marshfield and Frost's competed in the regional tournament at St. Joseph with the Mill topping Frost's 7-5 on the strength of Stu Dunlop's three run homer off of Roy Burlison who had come on in relief. St. Louis Budweiser won the tournament behind the clutch pitching of left hander Pete Kulenkamp. Marshfield had opened with a 2-1 victory over a great Cedar Rapids Modern Piping club, but that team eliminated both Frost's 4-0 and Marshfield 8-0. It was a satisfying year for Marshfield's longtime sponsor Gayford Crawford and the coming of age for some young talent like Doug Middleton, Wes Towe, Scott Loveland, Jeff Richards and Barry Marshall, all of whom would star in the next several years.

# TWENTY-NINE

## NEW GUYS ON THE BLOCK

The year 1983 saw only 24 fast pitch teams registered in Springfield. Al Hansen had opened West Town Softball Complex in town that pulled a few players from the city league but a lot of the players played in both leagues. The AAA league had seven teams entered. Bonus Frost managed the Tawh team with Charlie Slavens on the mound fully recovered from the snapped biceps injury. Magic Country Beef featured an aging but still tough Tim Buff on the hill being joined by hard throwing Doug Middleton and Chris Lane. Jerry Burwell still had a solid, experienced team with Wayne Ryan, Jim Maggi, Larry Cotter, Bill Helfrect and Steve Stombaugh all carrying big bats. Har-Bell had several of last year's Trailiner players with David Rothermel, Randy Nichols, John Maritt and Rick Young. Jerry Mallonee, John Carr and Roger Bumgarner supplied the arms. West Town supplied a team with Dee Prater pitching, and a new squad sponsored by Jenkins Diesel took on the circuit. The 1982 state champion, Marshfield Mill, remained pretty much intact but added pitcher Steve Stewart and catchers Mark Gann and Louie Bunch. This would be the second season all games would be played at Thompson Field in the Meador Complex and the crowds continued to dwindle at the far south side park. For the second-year teams who didn't qualify for the major state tournament could participate at the A level.

The top finish by a Springfield team was Magic County's league and district championships and third-place at the state tournament. St. Joseph Walnut Wood won the state beating a good Cape Girardeau Kelso team and the good hitting Schott brothers, Steve and Jeff.

The 1984 season opened with West Town's Dee Prater hurling a no-hitter against Magic Country Beef and introducing the league's first Kiwis, pitcher Neal Wardrobe and outfielder Billy McKinney. Bus's Casuals had good throwing with Roger Bumgarner and up and coming pitcher Gary Pringle. The Merchants had a young team with all three of the Marshall brothers, infielder Barry, pitcher Kevin, and the arm injured Lonnie playing third. The Henry boys, Joe and Gus, and David Frost were looked on for offense. The Beef still had their usual team with Buff and Middleton pitching. Ron Ghan's Har-Bell team had John Carr and Jim Evans on the mound with me throwing part time. Ghan introduced new players Tim Blasi, Billy O'Dell, Mike Snodgrass and Mickey Day to join older players Alan Potts and John Maritt. Marshfield had retooled somewhat, adding Charlie Slavens to the mix. They would join an ISC travel league with teams from St. Joseph and Harold's of Lexington. The three teams from Springfield playing in the major tournament were Marshfield, Har-Bell and Magic Country. Middleton pitched for St. Joseph Walnut at the state, which was won by Harold's and hard throwing Robert Newhardt. Marshfield had the highest finish taking fourth.

During an exhibition game against a St. Louis team Marshfield's centerfielder Mark Rice was being heckled by a spectator when he rapidly ran from the bench and scaled the high fence in, as teammate Stu Dunlop reported, about a second and began beating the tar out of the drunken fan. The fisticuffs ended quickly and they became friendly before the game ended.

New, young club Seeburg Muffler joined the league in '85. The team was put together by left-handed pitcher Ancil Buff and he was joined by father Tim on the mound. Tim had long been a great fielder at his position and passed on his long arms and soft hands to his son. Jerry Burwell and Ancil Fry had added some talented youth to their squad with Tim Blasi, Greg Smith, Billy O'Dell and Mickey Day joining veterans Steve Stombaugh, Larry Cotter, Scott Loveland and Ron Hubbard to form a solid team.

Doug Middleton

Doug Middleton and John Carr would supply the pitching. Lonnie Marshall's shoulder had fully healed and he and younger brother Kevin handled the pitching duties for Bus's. The Knights, Bus's and the Merchants, with Charlie Slavens and Steve Stewart on the mound, competed at the state major tournament. The Merchants was comprised of most of the Marshfield team and won the winner's bracket finals 2-0 over St Joseph Walnut Wood behind the great pitching of Slavens. Steve Stewart was in complete control in the first game of the finals hurling a no hitter for the first six innings. Walnut Wood scored four runs in the top of the seventh and won 4-0. They then got ahead early against Slavens in the final game and won the tournament with a 9-1 victory as John Younger supplied several big hits in the competition. The last four games played by the St. Joseph team were pitched by 21-year-old New Zealand import Greg Newton. Manager Dave Polsky of St. Joseph Herzog was playing first base when a pop up headed for the dugout. With both eyes on the ball,

Polsky rammed his face into the chain link fence surrounding the dugout. His nose bleeding, he yelled at his teammates, "Why didn't you tell me the fence was so close!" One of the players replied, "Because we didn't think you were stupid enough to run into it." So much for sympathy.

Polsky and sponsor Herzog Motors gathered a team of players over the age of 40 and won the Men's Masters Tournament in Lincoln, Nebraska. Springfield's Tim Buff and Ancil Fry contributed to the win with good pitching and timely hitting. That tournament would draw good teams for the next two decades, with a lot of player's wives ruing its existence. One wife lamented, "Just when I thought he had grown up somebody comes up with this over forty crap!"

The Merchants added Middleton to their squad for the Regional Tournament in Cedar Rapids, Iowa, for his pitching and added offense. Charlie Slavens won the opener 5-0 over Cedar Rapids Flex with Middleton launching two home runs. Middleton pitched the next two games, besting Salina, Kansas, 4-0, adding another home run, before losing 1-0 in 10 innings to Davenport, Iowa. They were eliminated from the tournament 1-0, with Steve Stewart losing to eventual champion Cedar Rapids Vigortone's New Zealander Mike White. The Merchants pitching staff had allowed only two runs in 31 innings and lost two games.

Eight teams competed at the AAA level in 1986, with Bonus Frost's Osborn-Merit Contracting team being the powerhouse. Osborn had three tough pitchers in Steve Stewart, Lonnie Marshall and Charlie Slavens. The team had a lot of veteran players although it featured youthful talent. Gus and Joe Henry were back after a year playing in St. Louis and, with power hitting Stu Dunlop and fleet Mark Rice in the outfield, they would prove to be a formidable club. The Knights had welcomed Neal Wardrobe back to Springfield and he would do the mound work with John Carr and me in a limited role. Manager Burwell had retained veterans Larry Cotter, Bill Helfrect, Steve Hutton, Monte Clithero, Donnie Haworth, Tommy Smith, Sammy Potter, Jim Maggi and Steve Stombaugh. The Har-Bell team also played in the major state with Jim Evans and Steve Hanson doing the pitching surrounded by the Towe family, Randy, Rod, Wes and brother-in-law Larry Plaster. Alan Potts and David McBeath also supplied solid play.

Harold's of Lexington had lured Doug Middleton to their team and, with Robert Newhardt as the other thrower, they sailed through the tournament. Harold's had been steadily building a championship squad. With the additions of St. Joseph's Bobby Blakely, Savannah's Kirby Hatcher and Springfield's Middleton and Scott Loveland to stalwarts Marty Albertson and Scott Sampson, they were a national tournament level contender. Osbern-Merit qualified for the regional tourney and picked up two big hitters from Tulsa, Phil Honeycutt and Mike Merrifield, along with Roy Burleson protégé Allen Colglazier from Pueblo, Colorado. The Osbern team won its first three games, with Slavens, Colglazier and Lonnie Marshall gaining wins. Colglazier was victorious in the winner's bracket final topping Cedar Rapids Teleconnect and Mike White 1-0. The Teleconnect team would rebound and win both championship games 9-1 and 3-0 with White getting both wins. The good news was that Springfield had been selected to host the 1987 Men's Major National Tournament.

1987 Tom Osbern Sales/Merit Construction

Front row: Fred Harrison, Doug Frost, Barry Marshall, Joe Henry, Steve Schott, Randy Nuchols, Andy Mallonee

Back row: Red Loveland, Bonus Frost, Billy O'Dell, Stu Dunlop, Steve Seevers, Jerry Mallonee, Denny Henry, Gus Henry, Tim Blasi, Joe Kitsmiller, Randy Peterie

# Thirty

## Grinder's Complaint

The announcement that Springfield would host the 1987 National Tournament created excitement in the fast pitch world and after only fielding four AAA league teams on '86 there would be nine teams now competing for the host slot. Rod Towe would play and manage a club sponsored by PFI and would feature Lonnie Marshall and Steve Stewart on the mound. Towe had secured power hitters Brad Beattie and Greg Turner to go with catcher Mark Gann, infielders Randy and Wes Towe, Glen Hayworth, and soft handed shortstop Mark Jones. Mark Rice would patrol the outfield with Beattie and Turner. The other favorite in the pack would be the Bonus Frost coached Osbern team. Bonus had assembled a young, talented squad that included Tim Blasi, Billy O'Dell, Steve Schotts from Missouri's Bootheel, Gus and Joe Henry, and son David Frost, with Jim Little's son, Marty, behind the plate. Pitching duties fell to Charley Slavens and Jerry Mallonee in the league, with occasional visits from Roy Burleson and Tulsa's hard throwing Mike Combs. Jerry Burwell's Knights team had John Carr, Gary Pringle and, when in town, Lexington's Doug Middleton pitching. They had a veteran team behind them with solid hitters Larry Cotter, Steve Stombaugh, Bill

Helfrect and Scott Loveland. The Har-Bell team would counter with left hander Steve Hansen and Curt Haden pitching and Mark Stratton, Alan Potts, Billy Slavens, Charley's son, and Kevin Rhoten suppling the fireworks at the plate. Northtown Sports, B and J Woodworks featuring the Brown family, People's Bank, and the Springfield Sting signed up to play along with an up-and coming young team Seeburg Muffler. Seeburg had been assembled by Ancil Buff, Tim's son, and he and Doug Gardner would be the throwers. Tom Smith would manage the squad and had good hitters David Wiser and Jeff Maggi, son of Jim Maggi.

The league was very competitive but, in the end, PFI and Osbern would both qualify for national tournament berths. Seeburg picked up young pitcher Terry Luster from Marshall, Missouri, and he proved to be a great choice as he led them to a third-place finish in the state meet behind winner Jefferson City Stags and St. Joseph Walnut Park. When a California region turned down their bid it was determined that Seeburg would get the national spot giving Missouri five entries in the tournament including Jefferson City, the three Springfield teams and Lexington due to their third-place finish in last year's nationals.

Springfield would play host to 41 teams, with all games to be played at the Meader Complex. The anticipated crowds were hampered by a week of rain during the tournament and the resulting game delays. The park board had city zookeepers train an elephant to toss out the first pitch on opening night, and brother Jim and Stu Dunlop were watching as the animal was led from the field. Just as it reached the concrete walkway a gusher of urine was dropped on the path. Jim Grinder, a huge softball fan and Roto Router operator, approached the large puddle. Jim and Stu gave a shouted out a warning to Grinder, "Jim, don't walk there. That's elephant urine!" Grinder grumbled as he walked right through it and replied, "With what I've had to deal with today a little elephant piss doesn't bother me."

1987 PFI

Front row: Berra Brown, Wes Towe, Rod Towe, Glenn Haworth, Randy Towe, Doug Jones

Back row: Greg Turner, Denzil Morris, Mark Gann, Jim Evans, Brad Beattie, Mike Egly, Lonnie Marshall, Steve Stewart

Seattle, Washington, Pay-N-Pak was the odds-on favorite after winning the last two ASA national tournaments and the '85 and '86 ISC championships. Cedar Rapids' Teleconnect had just won the '87 ISC tournament and they upset the defending champs 3-1 to open the games. Host team PFI, with Lonnie Marshall on the mound and Brad Beattie homering, pushed across the winning run in the seventh on an RBI single by Mark Rice to pull off a victory over Detroit, Michigan's Jimmie Moore. Moore had pitched Seattle to their '85 title before moving on. Other strong contenders were Decatur, Illinois, with former St. Joe and Springfield power hitter Ted Hicks and pitchers David Scott and Mike Combs. Elkhart, Indiana, and flame throwers Pete Meredith and Raynor Te-Wake, both New Zealanders, Lexington, Missouri, with Doug Middleton and Robert Newhart pitching, and a great team from Souix City, Iowa, Penn. Corp., with two kiwi pitchers, Steve Schultz and Pete Sandman.

PFI defeated two California teams before losing to another,

Guanella Brothers, 6-0. They were eliminated from the field by Seattle 7-0, with Marshall getting all of the decisions. Osbern had picked up pitcher Don Tillit from St. Louis and he threw them to a 2-2 record defeating Midland, Michigan ,3-0, losing to Reading, Pennsylvania, 8-1, topping Jefferson City 3-0, and dropping a game to the Plangers team from Michigan. Lexington won their first two games before being beaten by Elkhart's Pete Meredith 1-0 in extra innings and then getting trounced by Seattle 10-0. Penn. Corp.'s Steve Schultz was awesome, winning their first five games including four no hitters — one a perfect game, before suffering a knee injury in the winner's bracket finals against Cedar Rapids Collins Radio and pitcher Al Rausch. Sandman finished off that game but lost both championship games to Seattle by identical scores of 2-1. New Zealander Graham Robinson pitched the Pay-N-Pak team all the way through the loser's bracket to finish the event with a title and an 8-1 record.

The 1988 season would field eight AAA teams in the league with the top contenders being PFI and Osbern. Wes Towe would take over the management duties for PFI and would have John Carr and Jim Evans on the mound. Osbern could rally around pitchers Curt Haden, who was really coming into his own, and imported hurler Steve Coatney from West Plains, Missouri. The Merchants featured pitcher Duane Orchard from the Mountain Grove, Missouri area, while Har-Bell could counter with throwers Gary Pringle and Roger Bumgarner. Bus's, B and J Woodworks and Accredited Bail Bonds would also compete. Under the management of Jerry Burwell, Osbern/Potter would compete as basically an over-40 team. With Charley Slavens on the hill, the veteran team was credible on the field. PFI carried the Springfield banner the farthest in post season play taking second to Kelso Ferrel in the state and going 3-2 in the regional knocking off Kansas City, Missouri, and two Kansas teams, Salina and Topeka, with the aid of pickup pitcher Gary Pringle as they took seventh place. Burwell's over-40 team won its first two national games before dropping a 4-3 decision to Tulsa, Oklahoma. Slavens edged a Dallas, Texas, team 1-0 before the team was beaten by Carbondale, Illinois, to finish seventh in the tournament. Jerry Mallonee, Dee Prater and Sterling Price had added pitching support to their team's efforts.

The 1989 AAA league had seven teams sign up to play. The city had only 21 open league and church league fast pitch teams to add to the total of 28. Springfield's parks would be filled mostly by over 200 slow pitch teams of differing levels. Although slow pitch had siphoned off many good athletes that could have played at the fast pitch level, the lack of depth in pitchers was the main turnabout in teams. Some good pitching could still be found in AAA with newcomers Duane Orchard and Terry Luster added to the maturity of Gary Pringle, Curt Haden, Kevin Marshall and Ancil Buff and with some steady standbys like Steve Stewart, John Carr, Roger Bumgarner and Lonnie Marshall. Add old timers Tim Buff and Phil Wilkerson to the core and you still would have the basis for a competitive league. The Springfield Merchants with Orchard doing the pitching would qualify for and play in the Class A regionals, while Har-Bell and Osbern competed at the state tournament. Har-Bell would lose two heartbreakers, getting beat by St. Joseph Walnut 5-4 and Cole County 2-0 with all the opponents' runs scoring in the seventh inning. The decade was coming to an end and so it seemed was the sport fast pitch softball, but there would be one more influx of competitiveness and it would come from players who had thought their playing days were over. The ASA had decided to sponsor an over-40 master's national tournament and those old competitive juices began to flow again in those who loved the game.

# THIRTY-ONE

## BACK IN THE SADDLE

By 1990 the Springfield AAA league had dropped to only five teams. That had happened before in the mid '70s, but this time there were fewer and fewer teams in the open league and church divisions from which to pull talent. There were several good young pitchers in the twice-a-week league, with Lonnie Marshall, John Carr, Gary Pringle, Curt Hayden, Duane Orchard and Roger Bumgarner still throwing well. Jerry Burwell managed an over-40 team, with Charlie Slavens and Phil Wilkerson on the mound, but they played in a once-a-week open league. Of the five teams in the AAA league, one team, the Chameleons, were self-sponsored. Lonnie Marshall, along with four other team members Tim Blasi, Billy O'Dell, Barry Marshall and Joe Henry, would play with defending major state champion Ferrel of Kelso, Missouri, in the state tournament. Wes Towe managed Har-Bell with pitchers Hayden and Pringle available to go with solid players Alan Potts, Steve Phipps, Doug Jones, Frank Gallant, Brent Evans and Jeff Dishman. The Merchants had Duane Orchard toeing the slab, which made them a tough opponent every game. Potter's/Tiger Steel could counter with a pitching staff of John Carr, Jerry Mallonee and Ancil Buff, who would be helped by David Wiser, Tim Bade, Doug Gardener and slick fielding shortstop Howard Bell on the offensive side. B and J Flooring had Bumgarner backed by brothers Berrah and Danny Brown.

Har-Bell and Potter's/Tiger Steel would qualify for regional play in Topeka, Kansas, with the Har-Bell squad taking second-place. With the addition of the five Springfield players and two New Zealanders on the mound the Kelso team repeated as state champs moving on to the Major National Tournament in Mankato, Minnesota. Sioux City's Penn Corp team would become the Major Champions. The great Penn Corp team would suffer a tragedy later in the year when star pitchers Steve Schultz and Paul Magan would die in an automobile accident.

The Springfield Park Board made a "final nail" decision in 1991 disbanding the twice-a-week league and limiting the fast pitch teams to one night a week competition. Fast pitch throwers need lots of work to stay sharp and develop but now they would be even more strapped to improve. There were only 12 fast pitch teams signed up and they were split into two leagues. Of those, two were Men's Masters teams with Burr's/Magic country sponsoring both teams with plenty of older players eager to participate. From having over 200 teams in the '60s and '70s and probably close to 400 pitchers, the great game was reduced to maybe 20 active hurlers at best. The big news was ASA Men's Master's National Tournament was slated to be played here. By opening night 46 teams from across the country had signed up to compete. Players who had never had the chance to play in a national tournament were now able to represent their cities and states and to judge themselves against players of their level.

On one of the Burr's/Magic Country trips to play a weekend in Pine Bluff, Arkansas, youthful second baseman Jason Rader had tried to "run with the dogs" on Saturday night and showed up Sunday morning feeling worse for wear. He told manager Jerry Burwell he was sick and couldn't play. Jerry told him, "You're just hung over and you are playing!" Jason retreated to the water fountain, took a drink and quickly threw up. Steve Hutton had noticed and said, "That didn't stay down very long, Jason." The reply was, "It was just as cold coming up as it was going down."

The nationals was a fun and competitive tournament with Sikeston, Missouri, beating Fargo, Minnesota, 11-10 in the championship game and taking top honors. Lefthander Kurt Wilson, a cement plant worker from Hannibal, Missouri, won five of the six games for Sikeston and was named Most Valuable Player

The 1992 year again saw only 12 teams playing fast pitch but some stronger teams were evolving. LPI Paving had Gary Pringle and Duane Orchard on the mound, Seeburg Muffler had improved their lineup and had Ancil Buff pitching. Kent Leeper was building a great hitting team for Nelson's Sporting Goods adding former Missouri University star Danny Isemenger, power hitting Rich Carlson from Southwest Missouri State, Eddie Whitten, Mike Snodgrass, Jason Rader, Alan Potts, and wide-ranging shortstop Jody Brazeale. Jerry Mallonee, Steve Hanson and Tim Baker did good mound work to form a solid squad. The Christian County Merchants with Roger Bumgarner on the hill played their way to the Class B State Tournament, while Nelson's took fourth in the C tournament. LPI took on the Men's Major in St. Joseph and earned a third-place finish. Burr's/Magic Country won the first Over 40 Master's State tournament behind the pitching of Steve Stewart.

By 1993 the number of teams had dropped to nine including a team of young players from Marshfield, sponsored by Cologna's, with pitcher Larry Barnet. Bass Country Inn realigned and would feature former Springfieldian Doug Middleton on the mound for tournaments and the ISC travel league, and he would be joined by throwers Robert Newhart and Terry Luster. Kent Leeper's team was now sponsored by Ozark Chrysler and they ended their season by winning the Class C State in Rolla before heading to compete in the national tournament in Minot, North Dakota. Bass Country Inn was knocked out of the ISC Nationals by Toronto, Canada, with Middleton losing a 1-0 game to Canada's top thrower, Darren Zack. Behind the pitching of Steve Stewart and Charlie Slavens, Burr's/Magic Country had taken third in the Over 40 State tournament and traveled to Las Vegas for national competition.

The Falcons had earned an automatic bid to the Class B nationals in Garland, Texas, by way of Springfield's Heart of the Ozarks tournament. Gary Pringle provided the arm and Steve Phipps and Berrah Brown the power for the team. The Bass Country team was now called the Mountaineers and would again play in the ISC travel league. Ozark Chrysler, by virtue of their

Class C title the previous year, would have to move up to Class B. Har-Bell, coached by Wes Towe, would join them in the state competition held in Springfield. Duane Orchard had started the year with Har-Bell but then joined the Falcons, leaving Har-Bell with just Roger Bumgarner pitching. Towe had formed a solid defensive team with Justin Peebles catching, Towe at first, Aaron Snook at second, and the Hanafin brothers, Danny and Dana, at third and short. Scott Chastain, Kirk Wilson and Kevin Peebles patrolled the outfield.

I was asked to join the team just to have another pitcher to help Bumgarner out a little. By 1994 the ASA had added a new rule called the Designated Player. Different from the Designated Hitter, who could not play in the field, the new Designated Player could play anywhere in the field as long as he maintained the same spot in the batting order. Wes made good use of this rule as I was listed as the starting pitcher but he could use the good hitting Roger in the lineup, use him in relief, and he would never have to leave the game. I was listed as the pitcher for four winning games while only throwing one and Bumgarner did all the work. Ozark Chrysler had steamrolled through the loser's bracket scoring double figure runs most of its games. I took the mound in the championship game resolved to hold them down a bit by pitching around Isemenger and Carlson as much as possible. The plan worked for most of the game until I had to throw to Carlson with two runners on late in the game. He didn't quite catch all of a rise ball and bounced it off the left field fence, giving Ozark a 6-4 lead. We managed to tie it up the next inning and Bumgarner came on in relief to hold them until Kevin Peebles hit a ground ball through the right side to drive in the winning run. We finished the nationals with a 2-2 record with pickup pitcher Charlie Slavens and I getting wins and Roger dropping two well pitched games 3-1 and 2-0 in extra innings. In the game I threw I suddenly started rolling over my drop ball with good results so Justin stayed with it and we got a 2-0 victory.

# Thirty-Two

## Texas Two Step

As soon as we had returned from the Class B Nationals I was recruited by manager Gary Bass to pitch in the master's tournament in San Antonio, Texas. He had put together a competitive club with Alan Potts, Kent Leeper, Jim Pierce, Terry Lawson, Ronnie Ghan, Rondell Miller, Rod Towe and pitchers Jerry Mallonee and Larry Barnet. We set out on the long drive in two vans. Rod Towe, Terry Lawson and I rode with Rondell Miller. The other van carried Ronnie Ghan and his large cooler of drinks and treats for the road. One of our first stops was in Oklahoma for lunch and we pulled into a convenient McDonald's. We all ordered quickly until it was Ghan's turn. He kept studying the menu above the counter until I reminded him that all McDonald's menus were the same and he had worked as a manager for one for probably 20 years. That seemed to goad him into action. We invaded a restaurant in Texas for dinner and our entourage surrounded a round table in the middle of the room. An attractive young server greeted us and asked if we were there for the weekend rodeo in town. One of the more flirtatious guys quipped, "Do you think we look like bull riders?" With quick wit she replied, "No, I thought maybe you all were the clowns." That was actually a pretty accurate description of our aging group. That evening at the motel we encountered Jerry Mallonee and the large Alan Potts enjoying a beer in the sauna at the pool. "Rat" noted they had flown down and had just finished dinner. He claimed that "Big Al" had ordered the left side of the menu. He stopped by our room afterward to report that when Al left the sauna the water level dropped to Jerry's ankles! During our stay we had an opportunity to visit the Alamo and the Riverwalk. Ronnie Ghan made the mistake of putting his well-stocked cooler in our van so they could have more room in the other vehicle. We didn't see the other van the rest of the day and we nearly depleted Ronnie's treat supply! We ended the tournament winning a couple and losing a couple. I decided I would investigate the possibilities of assembling a strong Springfield team to play in next year's over-40 tournament.

With the help of pitchers Charley Slavens and Steve Stewart we were able to build a really solid ball club in 1995 combining some of Jerry Burwell's over-40 team with just turned eligible players. We were not as athletic as in our younger days but still talented, experienced and competitive. We had a good defensive infield with Gus Henry at first, Steve Hutton at second, Wayne Ryan covering shortstop, and Rondell Miller at third base. I had asked Mark Gann one time if any of the league's hitters scared him. He smiled and said no but when Stu Dunlop and Larry Cotter swung the bat it made a noise. I was able to get them both in our outfield along with the fleet Kenny Morris. Larry Cotter connected us with a new arrival from the Poplar Bluff area, Rick Gatlin, who had caught hurler Gary Holland for several years. Steve Stombaugh would serve as a solid designated hitter. Kelly Trotter was a completely versatile player with a slap and run batting style that brought good results. Charley Slavens would also sponsor the team and we grappled for an apt name for the squad. My brother Jim quickly supplied the name by using Charley's name, his business, and a nod of respect for his military service. "Charley Company" was the perfect title and we played under that banner for several years. We played in the ASA sanctioned state Over Forty Masters Tournament in St. Joseph and picked up Rod Towe and outfielder Bill Helfrect who had worn out the league's pitchers over the summer.

The fast pitch leagues held steady at 14 teams entered with

several being very competitive. Kent Leeper's Ozark Chrysler team won the Class B State and also participated in the Class A Regional tournament in Springfield. Jerry Burwell and Everett Payne continued their fast pitch support by co-sponsoring pitcher-manager Ancil Buff's team, which also played in the A regional. The Falcons were still strong with Gary Pringle on the mound. Har-Bell featured pitcher Roger Bumgarner and solid hitter Wes Towe. The DMP Rebels won the Class C State in Rolla behind the throwing and batting of Duane Orchard and Cologna's qualified for the C Regional.

We rolled through the state meet going undefeated before slamming Herzog-Polsky of St. Joseph 8-1 in the first championship game for the title. Charley Company ran into trouble in our first game at the national's in Minnesota losing to a knuckle baller from Cleveland, Ohio, 1-0 with a tying run being thrown out at the plate late in the game. The team bounced back with three straight wins before losing to a good California team and finishing in the top ten.

1995 Charley Company

Front row: Mark Helfrect, Steve Stewart, Steve Hutton, Kenny Morris, Steve Stombaugh, Kelly Trotter, Rod Towe, Danny Miles

Back row: Bill Helfrect, Gus Henry, Larry Trotter, Charley Slavens, Stu Dunlop. Wayne Ryan, Rondell Miller

The Springfield leagues held their own in 1996 with 14 teams entered. The crowd at the park had dwindled to a few friends and family members while the newspaper coverage was nearly zero. Of those 14 teams, two were over-40 clubs and one an ISC traveling team assembled by Jim Little's sons Joey and Yancey. They occasionally brought in Mike Combs from Tulsa to throw a game for them if they were playing in Springfield over the weekend. Charley Slavens faced off against him one night at Meador Park. With the score knotted 0-0 late in the game we had managed to get Stu Dunlop and Larry Cotter to first and second with one out. Dead pull hitter Wayne Ryan was at the plate so I put a hit and run play on to try and pull the shortstop out of position leaving Wayne a hole to hit through on the left side. It really made no difference as Wayne lined a double into left center to score both runs. The third base umpire remarked, "You guys are still really good." I simply replied, "You should have seen them 15 years ago."

Ancil Buff's Burr's/Magic Country Beef's young and talented team qualified for the Class B regionals in Omaha, Nebraska, and played well taking second-place. Charley Company traveled to Rockford, Illinois, to compete in the Over Forty Masters. We had added Dana Engle, Tom Smith and power hitter Rex Holman. We were prepared to tackle the competition but not the hoard of mosquitoes that greeted us at the ballpark that night. I can still see Bill Helfrect in center field swatting them off as he camped under a fly ball. We were rescued by the pitchers of Arnie's Plumbing/JM Welding team, Jerry Mallonee and John Carr, who shared their recently purchased supply of Deet. We won our first three games beating Peoria, Illinois, Portage, Wisconsin, and Mishawka, Indiana, before losing to Stockton, California. We came back to top Palmdale, California, before being eliminated in eight innings by Champaigne, Illinois. The 4-2 record had gotten us a seventh-place finish, while Arnie's/JM Welding had managed to take seventeenth. Rex Holman had brought daughter Tiffany with him to the tournament. She would go on to be a really good softball pitcher in her own right. It was a good thing she was along for the trip because at dinner one night in a dimly lit restaurant she had to read the entire menu for most of the poor sighted old timers on the team. The master's tournament was always great fun with teams who had fought it out many times in the past coming together for that last hurrah of competition. Jerry Mallonee had summed it up as being a huge fraternity gathering reuniting players from all over the nation who respected and appreciated each other and the abundance of talent.

# Thirty-Three

## In The Gloomin'

We entered the 1997 year by adding second baseman Tom Smith, versatile infielder Dana Engle, outfielder Gail Fredrick, and catcher Donnie Haworth, and I recruited Mike Larmer to coach third and be a capable substitute. There were two fast pitch leagues with six teams in each. Jim Little managed an ISC travel team built around his four sons, Marty, Yancey, Joey and Monte. They imported pitchers Mike Combs and Greg Fleeman for the trips around the state. Center fielder Mike Essick was a top player and contributor as they won the ISC state tournament. Ancil Buff had built a really good team named the Parrots. Borrowing from the red, green and white color scheme and the nickname of the great newspaper teams from his youth and his father Tim's heyday, Ancil gathered a club around fellow pitcher Doug Gardner, catcher Jeff Dishman, infielder Jeff Robbins, first baseman Doug Bennet, and Matt Anderson. Kent Leeper's Arnie's Plumbing and JM Welding was now pretty much an over-40 team now that excellent shortstop and hitter Jody Braseale had become age appropriate to join Alan Potts, David Anderson, Dave McBeath and Ty Laney as a solid foundation for the squad. Their pitching staff still featured Tim Baker, Steve Hanson and Jerry

Mallonee. Cologna's was a young team of former Marshfield baseballers with lots of energy and stalwart Larry Barnet on the mound.

We retained solid pitching from Charley Slavens and Steve Stewart, although Steve was having knee problems and every outing was becoming more and more painful for him. In that perspective, I relieved Stewart in a game against the Parrots when he was obviously fighting that pain. My first pitch to Matt Anderson was a flat rise ball which he deposited over the left fence for, as I assumed from the reaction of his teammates, his first home run. I felt that their overzealous cheering was a little over done as the good hitting Jeff Dishman dug in at the plate. Catcher Rondell Miller called for a rise ball and I tried to throw it up and in to push Dishman back off the plate. Instead, the pitch had some steam and headed directly for his left ear. Jeff dropped like a bag of rocks to avoid being smacked in the head. Suddenly their bench was completely silent as Jeff dusted himself off and looked out at me with a quiet recognition. Message sent-message received. The game resumed with a little more respect afforded both teams. That Parrot team would end the year in great form taking third-place in the Class B National Tournament in Orlando, Florida, winning six games before their second loss.

Our trip to the Men's Masters Tournament at College Station, Texas, was unremarkable, again losing two games early in the tournament. However, the new 45 and over Masters would be held in Springfield with 36 teams in the field. With Tommy Smith being too young to play, we had added Ben Upp to play second, Steve Baker to add some speed in the outfield, and placed Steve Hutton's name on the roster so he could get into the games at no cost. We defeated Fox Valley, Illinois, 11-2 in our first game before getting bludgeoned by the Memphis, Tennessee, Po'Boys 9-0. We snapped back with two shutout wins before taking on a very good team from Houston, Texas. We used the speedy Steve Baker twice to execute perfect run and bunts to put men in scoring position. With a runner on first and a right-handed batter at the plate the second baseman usually covers second on a steal. If you start the runner, the second baseman will usually take a couple of steps toward the bag. If the hitter lays down a good bunt and can run, the second baseman doesn't have time to get to first to cover and the first baseman must run in to field the bunt. Both times Baker made it look easy, never drawing a throw at first, both times the runner at second ended up scoring. We held on for a hard fought and costly 4-3 win. With the tying run on first and one out in the seventh game, Charley Slavens got the hitter to hit a ground ball to Ben Upp at second. As the runner barreled into Ben, he managed to get a throw off to first baseman Rex Holman who was spiked on the ankle by the hitter running to first. The runner at second had injured Upp's thumb and he was out for the rest of the tournament. Rex's leg was bleeding but he was able to continue the next two games. We got past Jefferson City 6-5 with Steve Hutton forced into getting dressed out and thrown into the lineup to replace Ben at second. He contributed some nice defensive plays for us.

Our next opponent was Black River, Wisconsin, with left hander Bobby Moore on the mound. Moore had given us fits over the years since our Horton's team had beaten him in the 1977 regionals. We managed two runs off him before losing 4-2. With a runner in scoring position, our last out had been a Bill Helfrect fly ball to the center field fence. As I walked past the bench on my way off the field, I passed Wayne sitting down as he was taking off his spikes. It came to me how much I had enjoyed managing him and watching his enormous talents and how fun it had been just having him on the team. I stopped, shook his hand and said, "You can still play, Dad." At 52 years of age, he was still remarkable on the field, always calm, never upset, always the professional.

Springfield was one of only a few cities that could still draw good crowds to watch fast pitch national tournaments. For most of the nation the game was lost to history survived mostly by the players still participating in the master's tournaments.

Charley Slavens' accountant had advised him that to legally take tax deductions for sponsoring he would have to use the actual names of his companies, so Charley Company became Artesian Construction/Builder's Glass. The league would remain about the same in '98, with two six team leagues of which four were church-sponsored clubs. The Parrots again had a solid team and won the Heart of the Ozarks tournament in Springfield to qualify for the Class A National Tournament in Decauter, Alabama. Lexington, Missouri, won the Over Forty Masters State Tournament for the third straight year, again behind the pitching of Fleeman. The national tournament would be held in Midland, Michigan. We added Joe Henry to the roster. Joe had been a part of the '77 Horton's team that played the nationals there and had lived and played in Midland for a year with friends Lonnie Marshall and Ted Hicks.

We played a league game against Cologna's and they were always tough on us with their athleticism and speed. They jumped on us early and got out to a 6-0 lead early in the game when their catcher bunted for a hit. Our guys took it as an affront, although I don't believe it was at all meant that way.

The next time up Slavens plunked him in the ribs to give notice that we didn't appreciate the slap in the face. He advanced to second and Tommy Smith informed him as to why he had been hit. It had gone completely over his head. The next inning, I was coaching third when I was verbally assailed by their coaching staff for the incident, accusing us of trying to hurt the player. I just told them how bush league it was to bunt for a hit when you are leading by six runs, but they were not comforted by my words. The next time we were scheduled to play them Charley would have to miss the contest, so I would have to pitch having only thrown a few rounds of batting practice early in the year.

After warming up, catcher Rondell Miller told me my pitches were moving so there was some hope entering the game. After our last meeting with Cologna's I was focused on the mound and hoping to gain some respect. It turned out to be one of the few games in my career when all the pitches worked, my control was good, and I had some zip on the ball. We defeated them easily 4-1 with their only run scoring on a steal when the batter grounded through the hole between third and short and the runner scored from first base. That would have been a good place to end my pitching performances but I was forced to throw against Arnie's/JM Welding the next game.

A change up too close to Jody Brazeale's bat ended up over the right field bleachers driving in three runs, and things went downhill after that. Between innings Rondell laughed and said, "You had a lot better stuff last game." Thanks, Rondell. I had taken a new job that year and my firsthand involvement with the game ended with a lackluster team performance in Midland. The team traveled to the Over 45 tournament in Phoenix, Arizona, without me as my traveling days had come to a close. But it had been a great 31 years of participation.

# THIRTY-FOUR

## FASSNIGHT PARK

All in all, the old park had not changed a lot. It still housed the concrete bleachers built in the 1950s that formed a semicircle around the infield from first base to third. It somehow reminded me of an old Roman amphitheater left to the ravages of the ages. The infield was now covered by mown weeds that had invaded the dirt from lack of attendance but bases and pitching rubber were still in place in case anyone wanted to practice there. The foul poles rose up in each corner but long gone were the bright white stripes of lime that had marked the lines and the batter's boxes.

I reflected upon how fortunate I had been to watch and play against the best teams the world had to offer. I had watched the famous Smith brothers from Springfield's west side — Joe, maintenance engineer at the Federal Medical Center; Paul, proprietor of a paint store on the then bustling Commercial Street; Walt, insurance adjuster; Larry, barber and airport employee; and Gene, salesman for Sears and Roebuck. They had played at the national level in the '40s and '50s for teams managed by the very successful Ed Bramer. I had gotten to see Tom Doyle, the most storied pitcher from Springfield during that time, pitch in an open league game. Well over 40 at the time, he was still imposing on the mound and almost unhittable at that level.

I had been given the opportunity to pitch against some of the best players in the sport's history. The most successful player was Bonus Frost, several times named to the National Tournament All-Star Team, who had garnered 14 trips to the meet in about 25 years of activity. He had participated in 11 of a possible 13 tournaments between 1970 and 1982. Larry Hale would be a close second with 13 nationals and set a national tournament record for 11 straight times on base in one of the tournaments. Left-handed slugger Bob McLish had earned a National Tournament MVP award in 1973 with an awesome display of five homeruns and 13 RBIs, both records at the time. They had been despised and more then formidable foes at the time, and my team and I had to raise our level of competition to have any chance of gaining a win. They had certainly more than earned my respect, and I hope I had gained some from them. Due to the many national competitions held in Springfield over a 40-year span, the best softball players ever to participate in the game had been paraded before me. Ron Weathersby of Clearwater, Florida, George Giles of the Armed Services team, Bob Barron from Aurora, Illinois, John Anguillare of Stratford, Connecticut, Chuck Caldera from Santa Rosa, California, lumbering Abe Baker of Poughkeepsie, New York, and Brian Sipe from Reading, Pennsylvania were perennial national tournament all stars. Probably the best hitter of them all was Carl Walker playing for Stratford Connecticut and Detroit, Michigan.

Looking to the stands from the infield I reflected on our team's supporters, always sitting in the first section to the first base side of home plate. My parents, James and Wilma, the Stewarts, A. Ronald and Maxine, my Uncles Delbert and Richard and Aunt Jo, Ples Spivy and his wife, Marvin and Willa March, the Henrys, Duke and Anita and their three daughters, Lisa, Nan and Beth, among many. I can envision my dad peeking out from beneath the bleachers to watch because the close games made him nervous and it seems like all the games were close. Also in attendance would be a guy Robert Rice nicknamed Willy Wire Hair for his apparently untamable locks. The "Wrestler", a muscular, hard looking man who we had witnessed tumbling down all ten rows of steps on his face and simply bounced up and proceeded to the concession stand. Cecil was a round little man who always sported a wide brimmed straw hat, blue slacks and white shirt and sat upon his pillow on the second row of bleachers. He was in attendance every night and after finishing his bag of popcorn would inevitably doze off until the games were finished. The white concession-stand still stood at the back of the stands right behind home plate. Leo Augustine and his wife worked the stand and Leo also managed teams in the league. The green press box that had sat on top of the concession stand had been removed but I can still remember Vern Hawkins announcing the middle game over the radio air waves until the late '60s from that vantage point, and scorekeeper, later turned manager, Jim Horton being bribed to change a debatable call from an error to a hit at the cost of a coke.

It has long been my belief that for several years the Springfield AAA was the best league in the country to compete in and have the opportunity to watch, play with and against the best players ever to participate in the game. I was lucky to have shared this experience with so many great teammates from Young Men teams to the 45 and over Masters clubs and highly respected and talented adversaries. As much I loved the game my devotion has been overshadowed by the likes of Sammy Potter who played with a jaw full of tobacco and constant patter, Alan Potts who was a stalwart at first base for over 40 years, Charley Slavens who I would expect to see on the mound if anyone puts on an Over 80 Masters tournament, Rondell Miller who started in the '70s and might still be playing and, last but certainly not least, Ancil "Spike" Fry who participated in fast pitch softball in six different decades and who would play right now if someone would hand him a beer and loan him some cleats.

I sat on the first row of the concrete structure and leaned back resting my elbows on the row behind me. The autumn sun is warm on my face as a light breeze brushes by. I imagine myself on the mound with the large crowd silent with anticipation. My right foot rests on the right side of the rubber with only my heel making contact. The toes of my left touch the backside and my hand cradles the ball as I hold it behind my back. It is the seventh inning, men on base and two strikes on the hitter. I peer in to see catcher Mark Gann hold down an open hand signaling for a rise ball. Umpire Artie Charle crouches down just to the left of Mark's facemask. My hand comes around and goes into the shelter of my glove as I position my grip. The forefinger nail curls and pushes against the ball's seam. I look at the ground as I deliver the pitch. It starts near the waist on the inside part of plate and rises nearly straight up to the batter's shoulders. He swings and misses. In my fantasies the hitter always, always misses.

# APPENDIX

As a point of clarification, the Amateur Softball Association governed play at the district, state, regional, and national levels. Many cities sponsored their own tournaments providing top-flight competition throughout the season. Springfield's "Heart of the Ozarks" tournament brought in top teams from all over the Midwest. Other great tournaments were held in Joplin, Jefferson City, St. Joseph, and Kansas City. Out of state competition could be found in Topeka, Kansas, Nashville, Tennessee, and Oklahoma City, Oklahoma and many other locations throughout the country.

# About the Author

Danny Miles was born in Springfield, Missouri in 1950. His family lived in rural Polk and Greene Counties until moving to Springfield in 1959. He attended Hillcrest High School and graduated from Southwest Missouri State University in 1973. Danny worked in the restaurant industry for over 30 years retiring from Wendys of Missouri after serving 19 years as a general manager. He and his wife Susan have been married for 35 years. Danny fell in love with fastpitch softball as a teenager and became an avid participant at age 16. While either pitching or managing he was active at high levels of the game including many state, regional, and national tournaments for 31 years.

www.ingramcontent.com/pod-product-compliance
Lightning Source LLC
LaVergne TN
LVHW051100080426
835508LV00019B/1988